PELICAN BOOKS

THE CULTURAL REVOLUTION
IN CHINA

Joan Robinson was born in Surrey in 1903 and educated at St Paul's Girls' School, London, and Girton
College, Cambridge. She took the examinations for
the Economics Tripos and in 1931 was appointed an
assistant lecturer. She became a University Lecturer
in 1937, and was Reader in Economics at Cambridge
from 1949 until 1965, when she became Professor of
Economics at Cambridge. She has also published:
Economics of Imperfect Competition (1933), *Essays in
the Theory of Employment* (1937), *Introduction to the
Theory of Employment* (1937), *Essay on Marxian
Economics* (1942), *Collected Economic Papers* Vol. I
(1951), Vol. II (1960), and Vol. III (1965), *The Rate
of Interest and Other Essays* (1952), *The Accumulation
of Capital* (1956), *Essays in the Theory of Economic
Growth* (1963), *Economic Philosophy* (1963; a Pelican),
and articles in economic journals. Her latest publica-
tions are *Economics: an Awkward Corner* (1966) and
*Freedom and Necessity: An Introduction to the Study
of Society* (1970).

Joan Robinson is married to the Emeritus Professor
of Economics at Cambridge and has two daughters.
She lives in Cambridge.

Joan Robinson

THE CULTURAL REVOLUTION IN CHINA

PENGUIN BOOKS

Penguin Books Ltd, Harmondsworth, Middlesex, England
Penguin Books Inc., 7110 Ambassador Road, Baltimore, Maryland 21207, U.S.A.
Penguin Books Australia Ltd, Ringwood, Victoria, Australia

—

Published in Pelican Books 1969
Reprinted with revised Postscript, 1970

—

Copyright © Joan Robinson, 1969, 1970

—

Made and printed in Great Britain by
Cox & Wyman Ltd, London, Reading and Fakenham
Set in Intertype Plantin

CONTENTS

CONTENTS

LIST OF PLATES

PREFACE

THE centrepiece of this little volume is the report on the Cultural Revolution which I received in Shanghai. The report was evidently carefully prepared. It gives a clear and frank narrative, including some details which I believe have not before been published outside China. It also gives a philosophical analysis of the events which it describes, providing a valuable insight into what those who are making the Cultural Revolution believe it to mean.

A number of documents which played a part in the history of the Cultural Revolution are included with brief comments. The translations have been published by the Foreign Languages Press, Peking.

The style of Chinese propaganda both at home and abroad (especially when translated into English) is not well attuned to our ears and the very fact that it is propaganda makes it unconvincing; the documents quoted here are of a different kind. They are appeals or declarations which themselves played a part in the struggle. They are of great historical interest and they give far more insight into what was involved than can any analysis by an external observer.

Some reports follow which were prepared from notes of interviews taken by myself and Mr Roland Berger.

The Introduction makes use of some paragraphs from an article published in *International Affairs* (Chatham House) April 1968 and from *Now* (Calcutta) 22 December 1967.

Cambridge, April 1968   JOAN ROBINSON

I

INTRODUCTION

IT is difficult even to begin to understand the significance of the Cultural Revolution through the medium of translations from Chinese, for not only the phraseology but the concepts in terms of which it is expressed are strange to us. What is the meaning of *a Party person in authority taking the capitalist road*? How can class war persist when there are no owners of private property to exploit the workers? How can the leader of an established government proclaim that *Rebellion is justified*? What are a *Great Alliance* and a *Triple Combination*? How does the thought of Mao Tse-tung make crops grow on a stony hill?

A New Revolution

The key to the conception of the Cultural Revolution, as its own spokesmen see it, lies in the Marxist analysis of society, refined and developed by Mao Tse-tung on the basis of his long experience of Communism in China.

Marxist analysis distinguishes between the *base* of a social system and the *superstructure*. The base is a system's economic foundation. The base of capitalism is personal property in the means of production, which yields rentier income and gives private enterprise control over economic development. Similarly, the base of socialism is State ownership and control of industry. A superstructure is the pattern of institutions, organizations, chains of authority, traditions and habits of thought which grow up in society. Inequality in consumption, the love of rank, status and power, untrammelled individualism and a social hierarchy based on wealth, belong to the bourgeois super-structure of capitalism; the superstructure of proletarian socialism requires acquisitiveness to be replaced by a spirit of service.

Accepting the dichotomy between the base of a social system and the superstructure, Mao Tse-tung shows how the super-structure may react upon the base: *Ideas may become a material force*. Contrariwise, when the base is changed, the superstructure will not automatically transform itself accord-ingly. Old-fashioned Marxists might regard this as a heresy, but that is scarcely reasonable. The meaning of a proposition depends on what it denies. Marx, combating the liberal ideal-ism with which he was surrounded, denied that independent thought, drawn from the blue air, can control events. Once the view that ideas arise out of material circumstances has been accepted, there is no sense in denying that causation runs both ways. If Marx had believed that ideas can have no effect on events, why should he have taken the trouble to write a book?

According to the Chinese view, Russian experience shows that a capitalist-type superstructure can grow up on a socialist base. When there are no capitalists to run industry and direct investment, the State develops organs to take over these func-tions, and the individuals put into control of them may suffer deformations of character sometimes even more unpleasant, from the point of view of socialist ideals, than those of the old bourgeoisie.

Sometimes a third party might feel that the embittered attacks which Chinese spokesmen make on Soviet 'revision-ism' are exaggerated and unfair. But they are clearly right in opposing Stalin's contention that abolishing private property in the means of production automatically creates a classless society. Soviet experience shows that power, privilege, and access to education can form the basis of class distinctions passed on from parents to children. Moreover, in trying to break out of the excessive rigidity of centralized planning, the Soviets and People's Democracies are resorting to economic incentives and market relations which, in the Chinese view, are inimical to building a superstructure of human relations in a genuinely socialist form. There is, certainly, an important difference between using profits as a criterion of success in an enterprise and relying on profits as a motive for activity; but the Chinese maintain that the first will inevitably lead to the second.

The Chinese Marxists maintain that Stalin made a serious and far-reaching error in asserting that class war comes to an end as soon as socialism is established. But the public is taught to revere him as a great socialist, whereas we think of him as the very archetype of the organization man. (His profile, so grim to us, appears on many a hoarding, as one of the prophets of the Old Testament, with Marx, Engels, and Lenin.) Khrushchev, who to us has certain sympathetic features, is the archetypal traitor to the Chinese, for he abandoned the international struggle against imperialism to butter up the Americans. Perhaps the contradiction can be reconciled by saying that Stalin saved the base of socialism in the Soviet Union, but did irreparable damage to the superstructure; while Khrushchev in trying to repair the superstructure only succeeded in damaging the base. There is a curious convention in Chinese politics of not naming anyone by his name until his status has been officially pronounced upon.* As long as he remains in limbo, Liu Shao-ch'i, the leading target of the Cultural Revolution, is referred to as the Chinese Khrushchev. For us this has wrong associations. Liu represented what we think of as a Stalinist element in the Communist Party.

The Party persons in authority taking the capitalist road, whom we may call the Rightists† for short, were accused of

*Cf. p. 93.

† This expression is used in a specific sense for those who were the

imitating the Soviet model. They were accused of carrying out their work in an authoritarian manner, developing a superior attitude to the workers, forming gangs to protect each other, and taking advantage of their position to gain privilege and amenities for themselves. They were taking the capitalist road in the sense that they obstructed socialism in the super-structure. And if a bourgeois superstructure is not pulled down in good time, in the end it will destroy the socialist base. The aim of the Cultural Revolution is to carry socialism into the superstructure and to root out from it all remnants of bourge-ois ideas and a bourgeois way of life.

In the Soviet Union, the old middle class was almost com-pletely wiped out. The new class developed afresh. In China, a great part of the middle class welcomed the victory of the Communists over the miserable, corrupt régime of the Kuo-mintang; they were willing to work with the new government in reconstructing the country; at the same time, they were necessary to it, since the mass of peasants who had won the civil war could not provide the personnel to run the adminis-tration, develop industry and, least of all, to man the greatly extended education services that the new régime required. Many middle-class people 'turned over' and believed that they had become socialists, but the change did not always go deep. In China the Rightists in the Party could find sympathy and support in the old middle class, and indeed were often of middle-class origin themselves.

The Chinese conception of class is not quite easy to grasp. The whole movement has been phrased as a class war between proletarians and bourgeoisie, but the old bourgeoisie were only minor auxiliaries of the 'Party persons in authority taking

---

object of attack in the Cultural Revolution, described in the Sixteen Points as 'anti-Party and anti-socialist Rightists' (see p. 91). In English conversation in China they are usually referred to as 'capitalist roaders'.

the capitalist road' who were the main objects of attack. Bourgeois intellectuals, except for those 'scholar despots' who were carrying out reactionary educational policies, are treated tolerantly in the Sixteen Points*, and special mention is made of the need to protect scientists and technicians who, though bourgeois, have contributed to national development.

Class is not defined by birth. An old mandarin or an ex-landlord may be an honorary proletarian; some of the most vicious of the organization men were once-poor peasants corrupted by power. Class is defined by a state of mind, and the state of mind is revealed in conduct. When the record of a cadre is being examined, former status as a poor peasant will count in his favour, and a former bourgeois style of life is *prima facie* suspicious, but in neither case decisive. He must prove a *proletarian* attitude today, not proletarian origin in the past, to be liberated from mistakes and rejoined to the movement.

Still less is class hereditary. Some ex-landlords have been found to harbour dreams of restoration and to pass on to their sons title-deeds and records of the lands they once owned to show them what their inheritance ought to have been, but this is not allowed to tar all landlords' children. When I asked a young functionary for examples of the kind of mistakes that cadres made, he took his own case: 'As I am a poor peasant's son, I thought I had no need to make revolution. I thought I was a superior person, and I protested against landlords' children being allowed to join the Red Guards. Now I realize that that was wrong. We should draw a sharp line between family and individual.' Some of the bad characters who infiltrated the Red Guards and made mischief turned out to come from highly placed Party families – a well-known phenomenon in the Soviet Union. The onus of proof is on everyone to show by his attitude of mind and his behaviour that he is a true proletarian,

* See below p. 89.

though as usual hard-headed with all their tolerance, the Chinese workers expect to have to examine the evidence more closely if the individual concerned was not a natural-born proletarian than if he was.

Political argument for the broad masses of the population must necessarily be simplified. To sophisticated listeners it cannot but appear crude. In the course of the Cultural Revolution the Rightists were presented as evil men. Certainly, under attack, they resorted to knavish tricks, but to an outsider it appears that they were not *merely* scoundrels; they had a point of view; it can be glimpsed between the lines of the accusations made against them.* It was something like this: Mao's ideas were fine for leading a peasant army but they are not appropriate to running a modern State. The Great Leap of 1958 was an irresponsible adventure, for which a heavy price was paid in the three bad years that followed. (The Rightists refused to recognize the return in increased production later enjoyed on the great investments which threw the economy off balance while they were being made in 1958, or to acknowledge that the communes have been vindicated by the continuous increase in harvests since 1962.) The Rightists insist upon the need for organization and authority. Every army and every industry in the world is run on the basis of a chain of command from the top downwards. That those in a higher grade in the hierarchy should have a more comfortable standard of life than those below is not only excusable but desirable, since it adds prestige to authority. The workers need tutelage; obedience and diligence are required of them; they are none the better for having their heads full of political wind. The task of industrialization must be carried out fast. It is nonsense to wait till the mass of the population are educated. We must build up a corps of managers and civil servants quickly; that means that we must draw upon the old lettered class, even if they

* Cf. p. 70.

were landlords or reactionaries in the past. In the arts, the dominance of politics produces a dreary philistinism and in literature a stupid black and white morality, smothering all the subtlety and grace of Chinese traditions.

Behind this lurks a more solid point. How can China stand alone in the face of the hideous threat of American aggression? Mere prudence dictates some ideological concessions to the Soviets (which, indeed, the Rightists would welcome for their own sake) to regain the support of a powerful ally.

Arguments such as these may touch a responding chord in many Western breasts, but in China today all questions are reduced to one: is this the road back to capitalism or on to socialism?

The Struggle

At every level, in the Chinese Party and administration, Rightists were ensconced in positions of authority. At the top was an organized group, evidently with wide ramifications, who were preparing to take power. There was no need for a coup. The President of the Republic, Liu Shao-ch'i, had been appointed as the successor to Mao Tse-tung in due constitutional form. They had only to wait for the moment when they would be free to set about running the country according to their ideas. Meanwhile, Mao was an indispensable figurehead, but the organization men could gradually get their supporters into place and gain more and more control over policy. This was particularly important in the field of education. In principle, education was being democratized but in practice it was building up an elite. The children of the old middle class naturally had an advantage over the children of peasants and workers as long as the old styles of formal education and formal examinations were preserved; under guise of maintaining academic standards, class stratification was being solidified.

The preliminary skirmishes against the position of the Rightists took the form of articles criticizing some literary works which were accused of making attacks upon the Chairman in various disguises. Peng Chen, the Mayor of Peking, had been leading a committee to discuss the question of socialist culture (this was the origin of the name Cultural Revolution, which now has a much wider meaning). He produced a pussyfooting report, without consulting his colleagues, which was repudiated by the Central Committee in a document published on 16 May 1966.* This gave a hint to a number of people, whose suspicions had been aroused by troubles in their own work, that there was something wrong on high. The familiar method of venting individual opinions by writing posters was used for a dramatic attack upon the head of Peking University. The publication of this poster on 2 June 1966 has come to be regarded as the first shot fired in the Cultural Revolution. The movement quickly spread to other institutions, and was soon followed by an outbreak in a number of factories of criticism on leading Party men in their administration.

The Rightists reacted sharply. Using the authority of the Party, they appealed to the biddable majority and isolated the rebels. Their counter-attack, picturesquely described as a *white terror*,† for the most part consisted only in abusing the dissidents and confusing their minds with the argument that to attack a representative of the Party is to attack the Chairman himself. In some places it was pretty rough. In some, the Rightists, getting rattled, only made fools of themselves; at one institute, for example, they ordered the service staff to cut off electricity and close the students' canteen. The rebels worked by candlelight and built themselves a cooking stove.‡ In many institutions and enterprises the rebels were pressed very hard, but they evidently had allies higher up. The Principal of Pek-

*See p. 71.   †See p. 80.
‡See p. 142.

ing University was dismissed, and the Party Committee of the city was reorganized.

All this while Mao Tse-tung was out of town. The only overt reaction he had to the situation was to swim the Yangtse so as to indicate that he had not yet got one foot in the grave.

At the end of July he returned to Peking; on 5 August he put up his own poster, under the title 'Bombard the Head-quarters'*; on 8 August the Cultural Revolution was formally adopted as Party policy. The Central Committee promulgated the guide-lines for it, which become known as the Sixteen Points.†

Rebels took heart; student groups organized as Red Guards flooded into Pcking and Mao Tse-tung put himself at their head. The movement, however, was still bubbling up from below, with little control from above. The limits set by the Sixteen Points, which are moderate and humane, were often surpassed.

From the Red Guards, the movement spread to the industrial enterprises. All down the line there were Party members in the highest positions at each level, who, whether they had organizational connexions with the centre of the web or had merely acquired a taste for power on their own, were ready to put up a fight for their positions and for the Party apparatus to which they were attached. Honest Party members at lower levels were bewildered. On the one hand the Central Committee had promulgated the Sixteen Points, on the other hand they had been trained in implicit unquestioning obedience to the direction of the Party conveyed to each from the grade above him. Many remained immobilized by mental conflict right through. Some saw the light, earlier or later. One important group, the municipal officials in Shanghai, joined the rebels in November 1966 as is recounted below.‡ A few

* See p. 80. † See p. 85. ‡ See p. 58.

declared for the rebels from the start and had to stand the racket of Party discipline for doing so.

There was a long, tough struggle between the Rightists and the rebel groups in the factories, rising to the level of city and provincial governments. There were serious clashes in some places where the Rightists had mobilized mass support for themselves. At one stage they resorted to what is not very happily called economism – paying bonus wages and promoting apprentices to full pay. (The expression is derived from the Russian term used by Lenin in *What is to be done?*) Groups of workers were sent off to Peking for a shopping spree until the favourite luxuries, such as woollen cloth and wireless sets, had to be removed from the counters. The rebels overcame this attack. Workers returned the goods and paid back the money to their enterprises. The effects of economism in Shanghai are described in Chapter 2. The fact that it cropped up at the same time in centres all over the country suggests that it was a move directed from the centre of the web.

The Cultural Revolution is sometimes represented as a Party purge. It is true that a certain group of leaders was deprived of power (though the sanctions against them were not in the Stalinist style) but the movement was carried out in a way unknown elsewhere. The rank and file in every enterprise and institution was called upon to criticize the cadres with whom they had been working. The people were to re-educate the Party and at the same time to learn that the Party was necessary to them.

In the Sixteen Points there is a clear distinction between two kinds of opposition to the Cultural Revolution – the anti-socialist Rightists and the remnants of bourgeois society. The attack is concentrated on the former – the Rightists in the Party. In the course of the movement the bourgeoisie outside the Party were to be weaned from old ideas, culture, customs and habits, but not personally attacked except when they had committed crimes to be dealt with by the law. Bourgeois scientists and technicians were to be protected. These were the principles of the revolution, but in the first uprush of the Red Guard movement they were not always observed; bourgeois intellectuals who had committed no offence except to *be* bourgeois intellectuals were subjected to cruel humiliations. Nor was the principle always observed that: 'When there is a debate, it should be conducted by reasoning, not by coercion or force.' Throughout the movement, the influence of Chairman Mao, and of all who followed his lead was strongly opposed to violence and disorder, but (as the account of the revolution in Shanghai shows) it broke out from time to time.

The treatment of cadres in the Sixteen Points lays great stress upon the separation of the Party as a whole from the small number of enemies of the Cultural Revolution.

In the third section those in charge of Party organizations are divided into a number of categories. Some are playing a leading part in the Cultural Revolution, some are terrified of taking a clear line. Some who are conscious of having been on the wrong side are afraid of being exposed. If they make an honest self criticism they can redeem their position, but if they try to cover it up, they will inevitably make more mistakes. Some are actively working for the Rightists. This describes the position at the time when the document was promulgated. In the fifth section it is stated that in the end less than 5 per cent of the cadres will have to be rejected.

The eighth section gives a summary of four categories of cadres and calls for the complete overthrow of the small number of anti-Socialist Rightists. The emphasis is on the redemption of the great majority.

Though the victims of the revolution were all 'Party persons in authority' no suggestion was allowed of an attack on the

Party as such. The first and most often recited of the quotations in the little red book is 'The force at the core leading our cause forward is the Chinese Communist Party.' Individuals who were caught on the wrong side are invited to change their thinking. The directives of the Sixteen Points narrow the target of attack to a 'small handful' and even they are directed to 'remould themselves through productive labour'. At the time of writing the disgraced ministers seem to be living quietly in some kind of house arrest, but in factories the few incorrigible Rightists are working on the very same shop floor where lately they strutted with offensive pride.

After 1 October 1967 when the most turbulent period came to an end, the greatest emphasis was on 'liberating the cadres', reconciling the rebels with those who had at first opposed them, and developing a new kind of relationship between the people and the Party, such as has not formerly been seen in any socialist country. The conception is that in the future, when the whole people have been imbued with the Thought of Mao Tse-tung, they will not allow the cadres to depart from it.

The adventure of launching the revolution and allowing the popular movement to boil up as it might was not so dangerous as it may seem, for all the while the People's Liberation Army was at hand, in case things should go wrong.* In the first phase, troops intervened only occasionally to separate rival groups who had come to actual blows; the soldiers were without arms, so that they suffered more casualties than the contestants. When production or transport were disorganized, army units came in to get it going and key installations were guarded to prevent sabotage. It was not until the end of January 1967 that the PLA was openly brought upon the scene and instructed to support the left.

Intervention by the PLA is not at all like what we under-

*Cf. p. 64.

stand by calling out the troops. In a typical case, (described to me by a foreigner in the institute concerned) where a dispute between rival groups was interfering with production (for normally production was kept going pretty well and argument took place after hours) five young men turned up with no equipment but some bedding, and held discussions and meetings for three days. Sometimes a reconciliation reached by these means came unstuck after they left and had to be made up again. (Another chore was to get the children back to school after their heady adventures, for which the army man would use the glamour of his name and enough exercise to sweat the mischief out of them.)

When the leading Rightists in an organization had been isolated, the main problem was to reconcile the various groups, each claiming to be the true supporters of Chairman Mao, that had formed in the course of the struggle.

With 1 October 1967 the dramatic period came to an end. Posters were cleared from the hoardings, processions with drums and gongs were heard no more. Reconciliation and reconstruction were the order of the day. This marked the victory of the revolution in its revolutionary phase.

At this stage Great Alliances had to be formed between contending groups. The process is described in the account of the Cultural Revolution in Shanghai in Chapter 2. Alliances had to be formed not only at government level but also in every enterprise and institution. Intervention by representatives of the PLA was often called upon to bring the groups together.

The next stage after the formation of an Alliance was the process of 'liberating the cadres', that is, examining the behaviour and attitudes of Party members in executive positions to see who could be accepted as a supporter of the Cultural Revolution and who belonged to the 'tiny handful' of antisocialist Rightists.

When the process of sorting out the cadres had been completed in any enterprise or institution the next stage was to call upon the cadres who had passed the test, representatives of the rebel groups, and members of the PLA to form a Triple Combination (in smaller establishments, the militia stood in for the army) and to set about working out a provisional organization to supervise the activities of the institution and to carry the revolution through to the next phase.

(It was at this stage that I visited China. The various reports in Chapter 4 date from that time – November 1967.)

There were many dramatic episodes in the year-long struggle up and down the country, many strange personal tales, many reversals and counter-reversals. Much is obscure even to those who lived through it, but the main line is clear enough. What took place between June 1966 and October 1967 certainly was a revolution, in the sense of an abrupt reversal of political power, carried out by a popular movement, as opposed to a *coup d'état,* an inner Party purge, or a general election. But it was a popular rising instigated and guided by the leader of the very régime which was established before it and which remains in being.

Red Guards and Rebels

The most picturesque and startling feature of the Cultural Revolution was the part played in it by school children and students.

They are referred to in the Sixteen Points in August 1966:

Large numbers of revolutionary young people, previously unknown, have become courageous and daring pathbreakers. They are vigorous in action and intelligent. Through the media of big-character posters and great debates, they argue things out, expose and criticize thoroughly, and launch resolute attacks on the open and hidden representatives of the bourgeoisie. In such a great revolutionary movement, it is hardly avoidable that they should show shortcomings of one kind or another, but their main revolutionary orientation has been correct from the beginning. This is the main current in the great proletarian Cultural Revolution. It is the main direction along which the Great Proletarian Cultural Revolution continues to advance.

When Chairman Mao gave them his blessing the movement spread over the whole country. At one time, it is estimated that two million young people from the provinces were visiting Peking.

They took a great part in the protests and discussions conducted by posters and home-made news sheets. They were allowed to criticize all and sundry, high and low, no holds barred. From Ministers to school teachers, they picked out all that could be accused of bourgeois thought or reactionary attitudes. There are tales circulating about Chen Yi, the Foreign Minister, known for his dry humour. One is that he had been sitting on a platform for some time wearing a dunce's hat, being criticized, when presently he looked at his watch, and said: Please excuse me, I have to go to the airport to welcome the President of Guinea. Or that, opening the quotation book, he intoned in the usual form 'Chairman Mao teaches us that Chen Yi is a good comrade'. The Red Guards cried out: Take off that hat. I won't, says Chen Yi: You put it on, you can take it off. There were some posters even against Chou En-lai, but these are believed to have been put up by a gang of young Rightists who infiltrated the Red Guards, or else by a group infected with anarchism and 'down with everything'ism for which Red Guards also had to accept criticism. (The view of some China watchers that Chou's position was seriously threatened seems to have no basis whatever. He was kept busy the whole time going round from one ministry to another seeing that the business of government was not interfered with during all the hubbub.) Violence was not in the rule book, but it broke out from time to time.

Why was the revolution conducted in this unorthodox way?

In one sense it was led and instigated by Chairman Mao himself, while in another sense it was spontaneous and unregulated. At any moment the Chairman could have used his enormous prestige to crush opposition. Why did he rely on the young people to open the attack for him?

The answer seems to be that, first, if Mao had cleared out the Rightists and attached the Party more firmly than ever to himself, he would have created the very situation that he was most anxious to avoid – a personal struggle for the succession, such as followed the death of Lenin and the death of Stalin. He wanted the succession to go to the people, that is to a Party who had been broken in to serving, not ruling them, and to a public that had learned to watch the Party, at every level, for signs of ambition, corruption and privilege sprouting again. The slogan 'Rebellion is justified', which sounds strange in the mouth of the leader of an established government, becomes the equivalent of: The price of freedom from Party bosses is eternal vigilance.

Second, it was impossible to know, looking down from the top, who all the Rightists were and through what ramifications they were linked, or to seek out their allies and sympathizers among the old bourgeoisie and ex-landlords. They exposed themselves by their reactions to attack, and by their demeanour under criticism or in confrontation with records of their past behaviour which the student rebels dug out, as well as by cruder indications, such as stocks of arms or the title deeds of old land holdings found hidden in their houses. (The famous case of the nun who was maltreated and expelled is explained in China by the allegation that Red Guards found a wireless transmitter and a wad of dollar notes in her cell.) A decorous, legal procedure could never have done the job.

The melodramatic and sometimes farcical aspects of the Red Guards movement have distracted attention from its importance in political strategy. By calling in the youth, Mao disguised the inner Party conflict and made it possible, by isolating a few top figures at each level while rescuing and redeeming their followers, to disintegrate the opposition without splitting the Party. The Rightists were used to patronize Mao, as a peasant leader, too simple-minded for the exigencies of politics in a modern state. Perhaps they are still wondering what hit them.

There was another aspect of the movement. Bringing out the Red Guards was killing two birds with one stone. For some years there has been talk of the problem of the third generation, the lucky children who take New China for granted and begin to think of what they can get out of it for themselves more than of what their fathers gave to build it. Their elders had begun to fear that cynicism, sloth, and self-indulgence would creep in before the economy was able to provide modest comfort for the whole people. There was some danger that trying to mould them by means of continual preaching would only produce a set of little prigs. Now another generation of teenagers and students have been plunged into the revolution and become committed to it. Running their organizations without the aid of grown-ups, and later on Long Marches, they learned more about politics and about their own country in a few months than they could ever have learned out of books. The education that the revolution gave to them was no less important than the political contribution that they made to it.

After power had been seized trouble broke out between rival groups thrown up in the course of the rebellion. (Actual violence seems to have continued longest in Canton, though most of the foreign 'eye-witness reports' of it would better be described as mouth witnesses.)

Once more the question arises, why did Mao allow it to happen? Why was the PLA allowed only to advise instead of to suppress the outbreaks by force? Once more, it was to let the people learn for themselves. The rebel groups had to realize that without the aid of the Party they could not form a stable administration. After asserting the right to criticize the cadres they had to find out that they needed their help before they were willing to accept it.

The spectacle of the head of a government (which the Chairman is in fact if not in form) inciting rebellion against the administration does not fit in with the constitutional notions that we are used to. This is what has most caused misunderstanding in the West and has permitted the press to represent the whole affair as mere chaos and disintegration. For the Chinese, who think of politics in terms of moral content, not legal form, it is sufficient to say that it is the Great Proletarian Cultural Revolution, led by Chairman Mao. Since it is a unique event, there are no preconceived categories in which to place it. To the historian of the future it will appear as the first example of a new kind of class war – a revolt of the new proletariat of workers in socialist enterprises and peasants turned commune members against the incipient new class of organization men in the Communist Party.

The Thought of Mao Tse-tung

Comfortable foreigners, however sympathetic, cannot know in their bones what it means when the young soldier, bursting with health and energy, tells them how his little sisters were sold during a famine to keep the rest of the family alive, or when the well-read Party secretary tells them that his mother was a beggar. They may guess, but cannot feel the wave of gratitude, at once intimate and exalted, that goes out to all that the name of Mao Tse-tung stands for.

The younger generation, who did not know the old China, are being steeped in the same emotion; all China is steeping in it, apart from the scattered few who refuse to be redeemed. There is an element in this of personal adoration which would be highly dangerous if its object were affected by it. But nothing could be further than Mao's style from the vanity and paranoia of Stalin's last years. The prestige of Mao is a national asset and he is using it, very coolly, to preserve unity in the face of sharp political conflict; indeed, it is hard to see how he could have turned the trick without it. The main emphasis, however, is not upon the mortal man but on the immortal scriptures.

There is pasture for subtle minds amongst the *Selected Works,* but the pieces chosen for the widest popularization are simply written to touch the hearts and confirm the resolution of peasant soldiers in the long hard wars that led to the Liberation.

The Thought teaches us that we must serve the people whole-heartedly, without calculation of loss or gain; that we must be on guard against the sophistries of disguised self-interest. It teaches that problems can be solved; to solve a problem it is necessary to analyse it correctly; mistakes must be examined so as to draw lessons from them; failure must be met with fresh determination. Problems must be discussed with others and mutual criticism frankly accepted, whether the problem is terracing an eroded gully, setting up a political organization or rooting out false conceptions from one's own mind.

The power that moves mountains does not lie in these unexceptionable precepts, but in the resolution simply and sincerely to carry them out.

All this may sound idealistic or even sentimental, but it has a very practical advantage. China still has long years of toil and accumulation lying ahead before she can establish an unassailable position as a great modern nation. High morale is much more economical than incentive wages.

The claims of the ideal seem much less extravagant in a socialist setting than they do to us. Of course it is not quite historically accurate to indentify self interest with capitalism.

Other economic forms are not immune from it. Besides, a modicum of self interest is indispensable in human life. Ambition and love of praise make a baby learn to walk. All the same, it is true that in a commercial society, everyone, not only the great exploiters, is under a constant pressure of competition which sharpens egoism and blunts generosity. When this is combined with a religion which preaches, Love thy neighbour; and, Take no thought for the morrow, public morality develops a horrible squint.

Moreover, the Chinese were well prepared by their past traditions to find a morally coherent way of life. Their religion was never theological, but based upon right conduct in this world.

A young Englishman who worked in China during the period of social disintegration under the Kuomintang, made these prescient comments on the generation he learned to know:

... one thing is certain: the collectivization of conscience which in the present anchorless state of society is China's greatest source of danger, will also prove to be her very precious heritage and a unique source of strength just as soon as new and more vigorous ways of thinking come up from the people to break the bonds of bureaucracy.

*

... the Chinese people's great flair for democracy is seen very clearly in the workings of the *pao-chia** system at its lower levels; for in its practice, the Old Hundred Names† give constant proof of their amazing reasonableness, tolerance, and gift of practical coordination.

*

* An organization of groups of ten households, through which the KMT controlled the populace.
† The Chinese man in the street.

But the real hope for democracy lies in these characteristics themselves and not in the system which, for want of a better outlet, now gives them expression. At its worst, the *pao-chia* system is almost pure fascism, and may well have served as inspiration for the system by which Hitler brought party discipline into German families. In its best and fortunately still most common form, it is no more than a democratic distribution of the class burden – a government of the people by the people for the officials. The Chinese peasant takes it because he is the Chinese peasant, and because, by nature of the society in which he lives, once he can read enough to understand what is going on, he *ipso facto* no longer belongs to the Old Hundred Names, but is a member, however humble, of the privileged classes.

The identification of literacy with privilege is still, after thirty-five years of the Republic and state education, the No. I enemy of Chinese democracy. For it utterly precludes that most essential condition of all democracy – not, surely, the existence of wise and privileged rulers, but the existence of a self-confident, opinion-forming, idea-generating people.

*

Losing itself in its work for the people, Chinese youth, afraid no longer of wearing straw sandals and overalls, or of being seen reading too much in public, will find itself. Patriotism will be based on popular national achievement instead of on half-baked uppercrust Westernism. Modern ideals of democracy and productive efficiency can be brought safely down to Chinese earth, and linked with the peasants' amazing aptitude for democratic forms of action – an aptitude now but half seen through the dark glasses of the *pao-chia* system. And who knows that a new form of collective face will not quickly emerge, under which everyone competes with his neighbour to get a reputation for unstinted social effort.*

It is precisely this that the Cultural Revolution aims to supply.

* *Fruition. The story of George Alwin Hogg*, by Rewi Alley. Caxton Press, Christchurch, New Zealand 1967. Pp. 107, 133–4 and 145.

A People's Army

One of the main issues between Mao and the Rightists, going back to the removal of Peng Teh-huai from the Ministry of Defence in 1959, was the character of the Army. (This episode was the target of Wu Han's play, discussed in Chapter 2.) The Rightists supported orthodox military conceptions and dismissed Mao's ideal of a truly proletarian army as a romantic day-dream inspired by nostalgia for the caves of Yenan, holding China back from building the modern armed forces that she needs. Under Peng's influence, the Soviet model was followed and even uniforms imitated the Russian. Lin Piao reversed the trend. At one stage, commanders were required to serve in the ranks from time to time in other units, so as to learn the soldiers' point of view. Now the return to the old Yenan style has gone much further; there are no badges and no permanent ranks; the necessary hierarchy is created by appointing suitable men to the appropriate positions of leadership. All eat, sleep, and study the Thought of Mao Tse-tung together. When men positively want to learn, military training does not take up so much time. The soldiers run farms to feed themselves and go out to help the commune members when they are short-handed. The old guerrilla tradition, that the Army are fish swimming in the waters of the people, is cherished more than ever.

No one has suggested that this peculiar way of doing things undermines discipline, for even the least sympathetic student of Chinese affairs has to admit that no army in the world has such perfect discipline as the PLA. Let us hope that no one is seriously thinking of testing them again as a fighting force.

Like many aspects of Mao's policy which seem extravagantly idealistic, there is a practical side to the concept of a people's army. Consider recruitment. The communes offer complete economic security, at the level that each has succeeded in reaching. No one will turn to the Army for the old reason – as refuge from misery. Selective service, when the boys chosen bitterly envy those that remain at home, is not good for morale. For the officer class in any country, however, the attitude is quite different. The men are taught to feel that it is natural for officers to be drawn from amongst their 'betters', who cannot be expected to rough it as they do. A conventional army preserves something of the traditions of feudalism. For officer cadets it promises an honourable career, with social status and a tinge of glamour. Candidates are not lacking, and a conventional army can pick and choose the most suitable.

This situation exists in China for ordinary recruits. Young men in the militia in every village are eagerly equipping themselves to qualify for the honour of being chosen to serve. Thus the apparently romantic idea of a classless army is serving a very practical purpose.

The concept that every kind of service is equally honourable is instilled into all ranks by the study of Mao's writings. The book of quotations is in daily use, and the little article 'Serve the People' is a source of inspiration. Nowadays foreigners are taken to visit a unit of the PLA to learn about the study of the Thought of Mao Tse-tung. A recent recruit recounts his case. He joined the PLA from junior high school and thought of himself as an educated man. He expected to be a tank driver, or at least to learn rifle-shooting. But to his chagrin he was detailed to the piggeries. He was so much ashamed that he avoided meeting his old school fellows and he could not bring himself to tell his girl friend what he was doing. The political officer got him to read 'Serve the People' and talked it over with him. He learned to feel that there is no low or high in service. He came to love his pigs; he saved the life of one that was sick by nursing it day and night. When his girl friend came to visit him, the first thing she asked was what work he was doing. Putting on a solemn air, he said: My work is very onorous and very honourable; I am serving the people by minding pigs. She laughed: Why are you so pompous? Why don't you say simply that you are working in the piggery? I don't believe that you have read 'Serve the People'.

When the PLA men go out to help commune members with the harvest, they show them by example and precept how to carry the Thought of Mao Tse-tung into daily life.

The Economy

As the next chapter will show, there were moments during the turmoil of the struggle against the Rightists when production was disrupted in some places, and after the Rightists had been dismissed, bickering between rebel groups caused fresh trouble. On the whole, however, work was kept going in a remarkable way. The great release of energy, the determination of the rebels to show that they were fulfilling Mao's demand to 'grasp revolution and stimulate production', and the possibilities of cutting out red tape and reducing the ratio of administrative personnel to productive workers, led to such high rates of output that many enterprises overtook arrears and fulfilled their planned assignments for the year two or three months ahead of schedule. Our China experts, of course, will deny that this is possible, but let any British factory manager ask himself what would happen to output if his operatives actually *wanted* to increase productivity, without demarcation problems or fear of redundancy, and would freely exchange ideas with his engineers about how it could be done.

In the countryside, far from impeding production, the Cultural Revolution helped to make the harvest of 1967 'the greatest in the recorded history of China'. There has been a succession of ever-improving harvests since 1962 and in 1967, though the weather was favourable, there is no doubt that high spirits contributed something extra. (Imports of wheat, which save transport in feeding the great coastal cities, are offset by exports of rice.)

No doubt 'natural disasters' will come again, but every year the area of land in which water is under control is extended bit by bit, stocks of grain are being built up all over the country and technical methods improved, so that the old helpless dependence on the weather grows less.

The old tale that the agricultural communes collapsed after the Great Leap dies hard. The communes were formed by linking neighbouring cooperative farms all over the country in 1958, in a rush of enthusiasm. They were invaluable during the three years of disaster which followed, for they formed an administrative network which could deal with rescue operations and control relief where harvests failed. But they had been formed very hastily; the necessary psychological preparation had not everywhere been made, and some extreme ideas, such as abolishing private plots and distributing food according to needs rather than on work points, proved to be far ahead of the times. During the bad years, reorganization took place. The extremist policies were abandoned. The team, a small group of twenty or thirty families, became the accounting unit for the distribution of income and the control of manpower; local fairs were organized to encourage private household trade. The direction of national investment was changed to favour agriculture and supplies of consumer goods were made available so as to induce the peasants to want to earn money. This might be regarded as a kind of New Economic Policy; but Lenin intended the NEP as a temporary device in face of difficulties, which was to be reversed as soon as they were overcome. The Rightists in China advocated these measures as permanent and wanted to push them further. Recovery, starting from 1962, and the fruits of the huge effort of investment made in 1958, began to show that the Great Leap was not a failure after all, but the Rightists were reluctant to admit it.

In 1964 the campaign for four clean-ups, in respect of political, ideological, organizational, and economic aspects of life and work in the communes, was a kind of dress rehearsal for the Cultural Revolution; it smoked out corruption among cadres and dangerous intrigues among ex-landlords, and it reversed some of the measures of the bad years – local fairs were given up, so that the sale of household products reverted to the Marketing Cooperatives and the regular State channels of trade. But in some places the movement was deflected into other channels.*

There is a famous brigade at Tachai, in northern Shansi, which is held up to the nation as a model. Here, as often happens, a cooperative that had been successful carried on as a unit within its commune, on its own lines. The terrain was the most hopeless imaginable – stony hills and eroded gullies of loess. The brigade set about creating cultivable land for themselves by the laborious process of building walled terraces on the hillside and filling them with soil. In 1963 they were struck by a deluge which washed away most of their work and completely wrecked their village. Refusing State aid to which they were entitled, they rebuilt both fields and village and then extended the work, so that now they have ample land to support themselves and to contribute to feeding the nation.

The Rightists in the Province found all the song about these achievements gall and wormwood. They took advantage of the four clean-ups to challenge the figures of crop yields put out by Tachai, saying that they had understated the area of their land and overstated their harvest. The villagers, saying: Is this four cleans or four dirties? stuck to their statements. Chou En-lai heard of the affair, and declared that national honour was involved – the matter must be cleared up. A huge team was

*Cf. p. 82.

sent in to measure every plot and count every grain. The brigade was vindicated.

They are now advancing towards some of the conceptions which were premature in 1958. They have simplified the work-point system and have one grand day of settlement every year, instead of nagging over them every evening (other communes, following the light of their example, have got down to once a month.) Private plots were given up after the flood. This autumn, grain was distributed by asking everyone how much he would need for the following year; only money income went according to work-points. Needless to say, these achievements were due to personal leadership – the Party secretary was a local peasant of heroic mind. But the example can be reduced to a system once it has been pioneered.

There is another aspect of the Tachai story. There are very great differences in the level of income per head obtainable in different communes for reasons of economic geography. This gives rise to 'socialist rent'. Moreover it sets up a cumulative movement. Land tax is negligible for an area where output has been rising, as it was fixed on the basis of yields at the time of the land reform. A rich commune saves and invests in land improvements and in installing small-scale industry, while a poor one struggles to feed its members. It would be politically dangerous to penalize the prosperous commune, and economically extravagant to deflect investment to the poor one. The Tachai example appeals to the poor commune to pull itself up by its own bootstraps and offers rewards in pride and honour that (once food and shelter are secure) may be preferred to anything that money could buy. Thus apparently starry-eyed idealism is found once more to be based on solid Chinese common sense.

The old socialist slogan 'Production for use and not for Profit' is not at all easy to implement when it comes to the point. A socialist enterprise in the consumption-goods sector has selling prices, the wage-bill and material costs fixed for it, and is instructed to achieve or, better, surpass a planned profit. It is impossible to set prices so delicately as to steer production into the right channels to meet the consumer's requirements in the best possible way, and directives in physical terms are even more clumsy. On the other hand, if enterprises are allowed to manipulate prices for themselves (as in some of the new experiments in the European socialist countries), the vices of a market economy – monopolistic competition – quickly creep in. The system of planning in China from the start has been more favourable to the consumer than in other socialist economies; the local branch of the Ministry of Internal Trade, in every centre, acts as a wholesale agent, placing orders with factories in response to the demand from retail outlets, so that the 'product mix' is continuously controlled by the requirements of the market. (Consumer's sovereignty does not always have a good effect upon design, for, alas, in China as much as anywhere else, the natural good taste of the peasant collapses at the first sight of industrial products. Only the 'national minorities' still keep up some resistance and insist on traditional patterns.) Even so, control cannot be perfect. Under the policy favoured by Liu Shao-ch'i the profit criterion was dominant and sometimes conflicted with human needs. For instance in a knitting factory, children's socks carried a smaller profit margin than larger sizes, so that under the Liu policy the shops were starved of them. To remedy this by raising the factory price of children's sizes and then subsidizing them would be the correct solution according to market principles, but it is much simpler for the workers to decide to produce them because they are wanted.

To take another example – shops in the cities cannot yet afford to run delivery services, but the girls serving in the vegetable markets make it their business to find out if there are lonely old people in the district who have no one to shop for them, and carry them supplies without extra charge. The commune cooperative shops send out to remote uplands when workers are too busy in the fields to come in to the village. In such ways the neighbourly spirit of country life is carried into commerce. The aim of Chinese socialism is to make use of all the technical achievements of modern industry without the dreary boredom and dehumanization of personal relationships that accompany it everywhere else. There is no point in arguing *a priori* about whether it is possible. They have got some way already and they do not mean to turn back.

The Arts

Devotees of Chinese history and art must hibernate for a while. Among the quotations in the little red book we find: 'Works of art which lack artistic quality have no force, however progressive they are politically. Therefore we oppose both works of art with a wrong political viewpoint and the tendency towards the "poster and slogan style".' But for the time being the latter point is not observed.

In the West the greatest art lovers are generally unbelievers, yet they can enjoy a Madonna or a Crucifixion, not merely with appreciation for its technical skill but also with a sense of communication with the artist as an artist. This kind of detachment from content is not possible for the young enthusiasts of the Cultural Revolution. Political content is all; the only form to be seen derives from a debased socialist realism which was imported by the Russians before they were repudiated as revisionists. Appreciation of their Chinese heritage no doubt will revive when the young generation have made the break with the feudal past so completely that they can look upon its works without revulsion. Meanwhile the museums are closed and the antique shops are out of business.

During the campaign against Four Olds – ideas, culture, customs and habits – iconoclasm broke out, in the tradition of the English Puritans. It seems to have been checked, but not before some harm was done. However, I can testify that the rumour that the Summer Palace has been wrecked is untrue – the only damage is that some of the little paintings in the long corridor that were felt to be glorifying feudal life were white-washed over.

External Affairs

The Chinese are sometimes accused of xenophobia, by which is presumably meant that they have a sense of superiority (damaged during the semi-colonial period) equal to that of the English. In the present movement, the danger is rather the reverse. The patriotism of the Chinese, which runs very deep, is so completely fused with socialist ideology that they do not notice that there is a national element in it. When the young things are singing of Mao Tse-tung as the leader of all the peoples of the world, it does not occur to them that their neighbours, who have national leaders of their own, might think them arrogant or fanatical. Trained to distinguish be-tween the people of a country and its Government, they are unaware that *Russian* feelings are wounded by diatribes against Soviet revisionism. Thus they make enemies for themselves out of pure goodwill.

In non-Communist Asia complaints are often bitter. China is accused of isolating herself by stiff diplomacy, sharply worded notes and fanatical ignorant comments on the affairs of other countries in the official Press. It is hard to know how much of this is intentional and how much a question of mere manners. During the period that they were on good terms with the Russians they took over the heavy, offensive style of con-troversy among Western Marxists. It is to be hoped that in the present campaign against revisionism it will be recognized and corrected.

We must keep a sense of proportion, however. Those very newspaper readers in Asia who are most indignant about Chinese pronouncements, learn that the CIA is corrupting their students and arranging to murder their statesmen with amused detachment. 'Of course, Americans are funny that way.' If the Chinese record in deeds, not in words, is fairly assessed, it seems that they take a great deal of provocation very calmly. (The myth of 'unprovoked aggression' in 1962 is, of course, still cherished in some circles in India and abroad, for obvious reasons.)

As for the diplomatic gaffes of the Red Guards, it is easy to see that the enthusiasm of youth, fed on a strong diet of anti-imperialism and anti-revisionism, would inevitably overflow the bounds of correct behaviour between sovereign states. Episodes such as the burning of the British Chancellery in Peking were certainly not in the programme outlined in the Sixteen Points. The authorities were evidently in a dilemma. Correct diplomatic etiquette demanded that the Red Guards should be checked even if it meant using armed police. The conduct of the Cultural Revolution demanded that they should be free to make mistakes and that they should not be confused by any contradiction of the simple doctrine that imperialists and revisionists are representatives of an evil thing. The solution was to let them shout in public and give them a dressing down in private for violating the strict injunctions against violence in the Sixteen Points.

So far as the campaign against imperialism is concerned, the Chinese leaders are calling more emphatically than ever for worldwide revolt, but they are also insisting more emphatically than ever that each nation must liberate itself by its own efforts. At the same time they have declared that if they are attacked 'frontiers would have no more meaning'. Who is willing to stand as a hostage for the U.S.A.?

Meanwhile China continues in her policy of refraining from all but verbal protests under provocations that grow more and more blatant. She has everything to gain by keeping out of trouble. No régime in the world is less in need of foreign distractions.

There is certainly a military element in the Cultural Revolution, but it concerns defence in the literal sense, not in the double-talk sense that we are used to. The PLA, for all its civilian work, is kept at constant combat readiness; to train a militia, to build up stocks of grain in every village, to inculcate self-reliance, so that local units can carry on when the centre is disrupted – these are preparations to frustrate an attack on their own soil. The H-bomb is a warning not to attempt it.

The military-industrial complex in the U.S.A. has an interest in representing China as aggressive in order to excuse themselves; it is not easy to make their case sound plausible. The Chinese authorities are building up the economy of a huge country, still poor but well equipped with natural resources, and now they have committed themselves to doing so without taking any short cuts, in a genuinely democratic manner. The Cultural Revolution makes the accusation of aggressiveness less plausible than ever.

The Way Ahead

To overthrow and discredit the Rightists and form new organs of power was only the first round of the Cultural Revolution. It was removing a blockage to the socialist road that now is to be followed.

The first necessity, adumbrated already in the Sixteen Points,* is to reconstruct the educational system, so as to cut at

* See p. 93.

the root of class privilege and to prepare the young generation to 'serve the people' with knowledge and skill as well as political enthusiasm. It is easy enough to denounce what was wrong with the old mandarin style; it is not so easy to establish the system of selection, methods of teaching, the syllabuses, and the tests of qualification that suit the new society. All this is in the melting pot with pupils and teachers experimenting together.*

At the same time, the new relations between the Party and the people at every level have to be accepted on both sides, consolidated and formalized.

The eternal conflict between the needs of organization and the claims of democracy cannot be settled at one blow. To develop a modern industrial state, especially under threat from a powerful enemy, needs planning, coordination and unified command. A government hierarchy working through a bureaucratic apparatus cannot be dispensed with. However much the leaders may be dedicated to revolutionary principles, authority breeds love of power and bureaucrats become 'bureaucratic'. The Cultural Revolution has swung the balance violently against organization towards popular spontaneity; how can it be kept from gradually creeping back?

The conception which underlies the Cultural Revolution is that the reconciliation of democracy with good order can be made by imbuing the whole nation with the ideology expressed in the phrase 'serve the people'. Ideology is necessary in any administration. It is impossible for every detail to be covered by a book of rules. There must be an accepted attitude which makes everyone know which is the proper way to decide individual cases. The overpowering emphasis on the Thought of Mao Tse-tung, in education, propaganda, entertainment and art is intended to develop an attitude of mind and habit of work that will put, as it were, a ratchet behind the achievements

* Cf. p. 143.

of the Cultural Revolution and prevent them slipping away. (Mao himself is realistic, however, and cheerfully remarks that it may well be necessary to have another Cultural Revolution after fifteen or twenty years.)

In the winter of 1967 the movement had turned inwards; the directive was 'We must combat self interest and eradicate revisionism in our own minds'.

None of the great religions has succeeded in producing a satisfactory society. The purpose of the Thought of Mao Tse-tung is to create a setting in which the claims of the ideal are not at variance with the necessities of daily life.

THE CULTURAL REVOLUTION
SEEN FROM SHANGHAI

THE following account of the Cultural Revolution was given to me in November 1967 by a member of the committee then forming the 'temporary organ of power' in control of the municipality of Shanghai. (Reflections and comments of my own are in parenthesis. I have shortened some of the standard phrases, such as 'the top Party person in authority taking the capitalist road', and 'the Great Proletarian Cultural Revolution'. The cross headings are mine.)

Introduction

All political struggle is a struggle for power. There have been three milestones on the road to socialist revolution. The first was the Paris Commune. It failed, but through it the proletariat gained valuable experience. The October Revolution was the first successful proletarian revolution. The Cultural Revolution is the first case of a revolution taking place under an already established dictatorship of the proletariat. Why was it necessary to carry through another revolution after power had been seized, and why should the Chinese Communist Party and the Chinese proletariat initiate such a revolution? The reason lies in the objective law of class struggle. Every revolution should be consolidated some time after its initial success. The class enemy will not be reconciled to his fate. After being dispossessed the bourgeoisie struggles for restoration.

(It is to be observed that the Communist Party is given

credit for initiating the Cultural Revolution and the enemy is identified with the old bourgeoisie while at the same time it is stated that the revolution was essentially concerned with seizing power from 'Party persons in authority taking the capitalist road'. In this there is a certain tendency to give propaganda a colour that will protect the Party as such from being held up to obliquity, but it arises mainly, I think, from the Chinese way of thinking in moral rather than legal categories. Proletarians are not only workers, but also all who have a proletarian point of view – ex-poor, and ex-lower-middle peasants on the communes, and all good and loyal followers of Mao Tse-tung's Thought from whatever social stratum. The bourgeoisie includes feudal elements, ex-landlords, and cadres who have taken a wrong turn, as well as the old literati and ex-capitalists.)

The bourgeois revolution leaves property intact. The proletarian revolution seizes property. The propertied class attempts a restoration. Many times in history a revolution has been succeeded by a restoration. In the Soviet Union, counter-revolution was defeated, private property had been transferred to the State, but they failed to make a Cultural Revolution. Bourgeois ideology was not remoulded and proletarian power was corrupted by it. A kind of restoration of capitalism was made by Khrushchev in 1956. (Here again history is coloured by Chinese experience. The chief crime of Khrushchev was in the sphere of foreign policy. All the blame for revisionism at home is heaped upon his head. The notion that it was Stalin who made Khrushchev inevitable is not enlarged upon.)

The sad lesson of revisionism in the Soviet Union gives us warning that removing property is not enough; the revolution must be carried into the superstructure of the economic system. In China, also, after the success of the revolution in 1949, class struggle persisted and reactionary forces were attempting restoration.

In the eighteen years since the Liberation the bourgeoisie have made three main attacks.

In 1951–2 they made use of the economic power still in their hands to try to deflect the dictatorship of the proletariat. (In this context the bourgeoisie has its normal meaning of the old class of capitalists and functionaries who had been dispossessed.) The Communist Party defended the revolution by counter-attacking with campaigns against the Three Evils, and the Five Evils.*

In 1957 Rightists made an attack in the field of politics and ideology. They made use of the remnants of political power that they had been allowed to keep (and of the prestige of intellectuals, who were still irreplaceable in the administration and the educational system). The anti-Rightist movement of 1957 was a defence against this attack.

In the three bitter years of harvest failures and the withdrawal of Soviet aid, 1959, 1960 and 1961, the bourgeoisie launched an unprecedented great attack. (This time Party persons in authority were responsible rather than the old bourgeoisie.) They attacked in the field of ideology. They used the radio and the Press to make propaganda for restoration. (Here restoration means revisionism on the Khrushchev model – the use of economic incentives, encouragement of private trade and so forth.) They proposed many political ideas which had the tendency of restoring capitalism, and many of their schemes were wholly or partially carried into effect. During this time the influence of certain Party persons in authority who were taking the capitalist road came to a high tide. In some

---

*The Three Evils (san fan) were vices amongst government officials – corruption, waste and bureaucracy. The Five Evils (wu fan) were vices of the capitalist business men who, at that time, were not yet absorbed into the socialist system – bribery of government personnel, tax evasion, theft of state property, cheating on government contracts and stealing economic information.

enterprises power was usurped by them. It was for this reason that the Cultural Revolution was necessary. It is a struggle for political power, that is, for the seizure of power from these Party persons in authority. Chairman Mao's pronouncement: To rebel is justified, means, in this case, to seize power from the top Party person.

Marxism teaches that the proletariat must seize power from the bourgeois state. This is the first stage of the establishment of socialism. Under the leadership of Lenin and Stalin, the proletarian revolution was successful against the bourgeoisie. This was the second stage. Under the leadership of Mao Tse-tung, a revolution has been made in a semi-feudal, semi-colonial society. The third stage is the Cultural Revolution carried out under the dictatorship of the proletariat, in order to consolidate it. The need for a seizure of power is limited to certain spheres and certain regions, not in the whole of society. The proletarian revolution reverses the restoration at the points where power had been usurped by the top Party person. It is a new creation, without any historical precedent.

Shanghai was the focus of the Cultural Revolution. The struggle in Shanghai was very sharp. The forces on both sides were strong. After Liberation, class conflict did not come to an end. On the one hand there was a large industrial working class with high political consciousness. The administration was led by the Mayor, Ko Chin-sze, who was a true proletarian and a true follower of Mao Tse-tung. On the other hand the old bourgeoisie and the national capitalists who were allowed to work with the revolutionary régime were numerous and their experience in running industry gave them power and influence. Party persons taking the capitalist road were well entrenched. Chao Ti-chu who succeeded Ko as mayor after his death in April 1965, and Chen Pei-shien, who then moved up from second to first secretary of the city Party Committee, turned out to be strong and bitter adversaries of

Chairman Mao's policies. In Shanghai, the Cultural Revolution was the final great battle between these opposing forces. The battle was fought out in three stages.

Skirmishes in the Field of Culture

As Chairman Mao has pointed out, a political movement must begin with the formation of public opinion. This is just as much true for the counter-revolutionaries as it is for the proletariat. In 1963 bourgeois ideology was being attacked by the transformation of Peking opera in which Chiang Ching (the Chairman's wife) played a leading part. (The new operas are concerned with stories taken from the period of the long and multifarious struggles that led up to Liberation, and contemporary themes such as the Korean War. Abandoning the subtlety and refinement of a palace art, they depict heroes and villains in strong, simple lines. They are extremely popular, and evidently have a powerful appeal to their audiences. The old opera was concerned with emperors, mandarins, court beauties and tales of magic. The common people in it were mainly treated as low-life comics. It glamorized feudalism with its fascinating technique and gorgeous dress. The young generation had no sympathy for it and the exquisite old art was already withering for lack of audiences.) The old opera was propaganda for the restoration of capitalism. The very fact that it was used in the political struggle on the bourgeois side has led to its destruction.

The struggle was sharp. After one of the new operas – *The Lakeside Village* – had been shown in Peking, Peng Chen, the Mayor, dispersed the company so that it could not play in other parts of the country. Chiang Ching came down to Shanghai so as to arrange some productions there. Chao and Chen tried to boycott them. When invited to see them, they refused to comment, saying they were not experts and had no opinion to offer. They encouraged performances of old operas to be kept going and prevented public performances of the new. When they could not avoid attending a private performance, they put about opinions: This is neither a horse nor an ass – It has no more taste than water – It is just an ordinary play with a few songs. Chiang Ching replied at the same level: All operas are dramas with songs – Sweets and wine are made with water – and so forth. (The following is an example of the conflict between theatrical standards and the need to simplify for an unsophisticated audience. In *Taking the Bandit's Stronghold* a soldier of the People's Liberation Army disguises himself as a bandit, joins the gang and hands over the stronghold when the PLA attacks. Although supposed to be deceiving the bandits, his costume on the stage distinguishes him clearly as a heroic figure.) The critics claimed that the hero of *Taking the Bandit's Stronghold* ought to be disguised properly to look like a bandit. They kept up an insidious underhand struggle against the new operas (which, however, were enjoying a great success with the public).

The struggle in the cultural field continued and grew sharper. In 1965, the Chairman called for the repudiation of Wu Han, the Vice-Mayor of Peking, who was publishing articles making covert attacks on Mao Tse-tung's policies. His play *Hai Jui Dismissed from Office* (in the form of an episode from the history of the Ming Court involving the dismissal of a 'righteous official') was whitewashing the Minister of Defence, Peng Teh-huai, who had been demoted in 1959. (He was a supporter of the Russian alliance and presumably had connexions with the anti-Mao faction in the Central Committee. To ensure the loyalty of the PLA to the Chairman was an essential pre-condition for launching the Cultural Revolution. The appointment of Lin Piao as Minister of Defence in September 1959 was an important step.) Chiang Ching (the Chairman's wife) tried to get articles written against Wu Han. But he was under the protection of Peng Chen, the Mayor of Peking (a member of the Political Bureau of the secretariat of the Party) and writers were afraid to oppose him. Failing in Peking, Chiang Ching came down to Shanghai and there found volunteers for the task, Chang Chun-chao and Yao Wen-yuan. They showed considerable courage, for the danger of assassination could not be excluded. The article criticizing Wu Han's play was written in secret. But somehow Peng Chen (Mayor of Peking) came to hear of it and demanded to see it. His next dodge was to accept the article provided the fourth paragraph was deleted. This paragraph contained the whole point of the argument – that Wu Han was covertly attacking Chairman Mao. Chiang Ching refused to allow it to be cut out. Peng Chen would not allow the article to be published in Peking. It was finally published in Shanghai in November 1965, Yao Wen-yuan being named as the author.

This raised the curtain on the Cultural Revolution. Peng Chen was now alarmed. His first reaction was to use the hard line. He rang up Chang Chun-chao and asked him 'Where is your Party spirit?' At the same time he tried the soft line. In a circular on the problem of Socialist culture, issued on 6 February 1966, he tried to pass off the whole problem as a purely academic question, concerned with how historical figures should be evaluated and the nature of morality in the feudal age. He tried to deprive the issue of relevance to politics today and turn it into a discussion of history. This document was written behind the Chairman's back, but Liu Shao-ch'i used his authority to make it an official Central Committee document. The decision to publish it was taken in Liu Shao-ch'i's house. The Party Secretary and the Mayor of Shanghai, Chen and Chao, found this very valuable. The newspapers in Shanghai were instructed to deflect the argument into an academic discussion.

Chang Chun-chao went to Peking and reported to the Central Committee that the 6 February circular was mistaken and showed a wrong orientation. Chang and Yao disregarded its directive and organized articles to continue the criticism of 'Hai Jui' in political terms. This began to alert the working class. The movement of criticism went deep and it became clear that Wu Han had the powerful backing of the Mayor of Peking. In April 1966, the Mayor tried a new trick – sacrificing a knight to save the queen. He sacrificed his subordinate Teng To (the editor of *Peking Daily* and other journals), saying that he had been the main supporter of Wu Han, thus directing the fire away from himself. In May, Yao Wen-yuan (the author of the November article) published an exposure of the series of tales, 'Three Family Village', showing that Teng To and his associates had used them to make scarcely veiled attacks on Mao Tse-tung, and that Teng To himself had a powerful backer – the allusion was to Peng Chen. In Shanghai, Chen and Chao tried to suppress Yao's article and would not let it be broadcast. Soon they changed their tactics and pretended to agree that the repudiation of the erroneous line should go on and tried to bring it under their own control and to claim credit for it. They declared that criticism of 'Three Family Village' should be made by the Party Committee, not under Yao's name in the public press.

In April 1965, the beloved Mayor of Shanghai, Ko Chin-sze, had died (he had been out of action through illness for some time) and Chao became Mayor; Chen Pei-shien moved up into his place as First Secretary of the Party Committee. They now had the Government of Shanghai in their pocket. They tried to gild themselves with the success and the popularity of the old Mayor, but they were being to a certain extent exposed by their own actions and the masses began to be mobilized against them.

This was the end of the first stage of the Cultural Revolution. The struggle now reached the level of Party organization.

The Struggle Begins

The second stage of the Cultural Revolution, the active struggle, can be divided into three parts.

On 16 May the Central Committee issued a circular repudiating Peng Chen's report of 6 February.* This circular was drafted and approved by Chairman Mao himself. It refers to 'those like Khrushchev who nestle beside us'. At this stage, Party members generally took this to be aimed no higher than Peng Chen, the Mayor of Peking; in reality it pointed to the top Party person, Liu Shao-ch'i, as the leader of the revisionists. The 16 May circular alerted many cadres to what was going on, and the conflict became widespread. The famous big character poster against Lu Ping, the Principal of Peking University was published on 2 June 1966. Mao Tse-tung had left Peking (ostensibly) for one of his usual tours of inspection. He commented that this was the first Marxist-Leninist big character poster, because it raised the question of taking power in an organization. It had the spirit of the Paris Commune. He instructed that it should be published in the press. It was broadcast all over the country. The Great Debate was now opened. In the streets of Shanghai five or six thousand posters appeared.

The revisionists were now thoroughly alarmed. Liu Shao-ch'i (the President) and Teng Hsiao-ping (the First Secretary of the Party, usually referred to as 'the other top Party person taking the capitalist road') tried a thousand ways to dodge and counter-attack. While Mao was out of Peking, they were in power. They decreed that posters should distinguish between intra-Party and extra-Party matters, and that Party affairs should not be discussed in public. This would have

* See p. 71.

smothered the debate, for if the Cultural Revolution could not expose the top Party persons, it could not do anything. They sent work teams into institutions where rebels were active and used the Party Committees in the universities to try to curb them. All over the country they used the authority of Party Committees to suppress the rebel movement. They took advantage of minor mistakes that rebels made to treat them as anti-Party, anti-socialist and so forth. They argued that if you oppose the authority of the head of a work team, you are opposing the Party, and if you oppose the Party, you oppose Chairman Mao. Rebels were branded as counter-revolutionaries.

In Shanghai, Chao and Chen, in the same way, were fighting on the reactionary line with all the authority they could command. They claimed that the leadership of the Shanghai Party Committee cannot be incorrect and must be followed. They had two resources. First, they could draw upon the capital of goodwill that had been built up by progress under the old Mayor, for which they claimed credit; secondly they could pretend that it was they who had initiated the Cultural Revolution in Shanghai and it was they who were the followers of Chairman Mao's line. They claimed that the Municipal Party Committee was supporting the Central Committee and that to oppose them was to oppose the Chairman himself. They tried to turn the spearhead of the rebellion against the masses; those who had made minor mistakes were treated as the main enemy.

The weaknesses of the rebels were turned against them. They were not wholly clear in their views on economic and moral questions; this permitted the revisionists to confuse the minds of the rank and file. In some enterprises, 50 per cent of the workers rallied to the Party leaders, in some as many as 80 per cent. The struggle raged through June and July. This was the first part of the second stage of the Cultural Revolution.

Chairman Mao Intervenes

At the end of July Chairman Mao returned to Peking. He found that the Cultural Revolution had been partially smothered. It was clear that Liu Shao-ch'i was taking the bourgeois reactionary line. (This cannot have been news to the Chairman.) The masses were being attacked, and Liu was relying on the Party to fight on his side. They attacked the many in order to protect the few.

The Chairman immediately called a meeting of the Central Committee. The Eleventh Plenary Session of the Eighth Party Committee, on 8 August, promulgated its 'Decision Concerning the Great Proletarian Cultural Revolution', popularly known as the Sixteen Points.* (No account has yet leaked out of what was Liu's demeanour at this meeting.)

Mao Tse-tung put up his own poster 'Bombard the Head-quarters'.† Without naming names, this made it clear that Liu was the leader of the reactionaries. Mao Tse-tung's line was to have faith in the masses, to respect their initiative, and to accept the risk of disturbances without timidity.

The high tide of debate and rebellion rose again. The flame, which had been almost stamped out, was rekindled.

On 18 August at a mass rally of Red Guards, Mao Tse-tung put their red band on his own arm. The movement spread all over the country. The Red Guards were everywhere attacking the Four Olds – ideas, culture, customs and habits.

Chairman Mao had said at the meeting of the Central Committee that a number of persons in authority would refuse to carry out the Sixteen Points. The Minister and Vice-Minister of Propaganda had been dismissed in June. Tao Chu who was appointed in their place took up a pose on the ultra left. He turned out to be no less reactionary than those who had been dismissed, which caused great confusion for a certain

* See p. 84.   † See p. 80.

time. Liu and Teng had been obliged to stand aside, but Tao carried on until he was dismissed at the beginning of January 1967.

In Shanghai, Chao and others maintained their links with him and kept up the fight for the bourgeois reactionary line. Chao was at the Eleventh Plenary. When he returned to Shanghai to report, he gave a dry account of the proceedings, taking only half an hour, merely mentioning the date, the time, and the list of speakers, without saying anything about the substance of the meeting. He and Chen tried to suppress Mao's poster, 'Bombard the Headquarters'. Nothing was known of it in Shanghai until Red Guards from Peking brought it there at the end of August. They then put about a rumour that it was a forgery. Many workers and cadres were taken in.

From this the Red Guards began to realize that there was something seriously wrong with the Party Committee of Shanghai. They began to 'bombard the headquarters'. Many workers and students who had been deceived by the reactionaries rallied to defend the Municipal Party Committee. There were crowds round the Party Committee offices, day and night, debating and arguing. Chao and Chen, the Mayor and First Secretary, backed up by their following of cadres, accused the students from Peking of being of bad origin, landlords' children, who were the real reactionaries. They egged on the workers to fight the Red Guards. This was too much – more and more workers began to realize that there must be something wrong and turned over to the students' side.

At the end of August, a revolutionary student group was formed in Shanghai.* In Chinese history, students have always been in the vanguard of revolution. From August to October the struggle raged. But the top Party persons in authority in Shanghai held obstinately to the reactionary line.

* See p. 143.

The Struggle Goes On

The end of the second part of stage two of the Cultural Revolution was marked by a meeting of the Central Committee called by Chairman Mao in October. At this meeting there were important speeches by Lin Piao (the Vice-Premier and Minister of Defence, who was being built up in the popular mind as Mao's closest supporter and heir presumptive) and by Chen Po-ta (the editor of the Party journal *Red Flag*). Lin Piao appealed for struggle against the bourgeois line and for support for the rebels. Liu and Teng had to make a self criticism, but it was not accepted as being sincere. The speeches by Lin Piao and by Chen Po-ta were given out to the Red Guards so as to frustrate the boycott which had been successful last time. Chen and Chao in Shanghai once more attempted to suppress the speeches, but finally they got out to the masses.

The struggle raged even more fiercely through December. After the meeting of the Central Committee, the workers realized how they had been deceived. At the beginning of November a Headquarters was set up to coordinate the various rebel groups. The industrial working class is the main force in a revolutionary movement. As soon as the workers were roused, the situation changed rapidly. The reactionaries were now thoroughly alarmed. They preached to the workers that they must not waste time on politics. They quoted Mao's directive in the Sixteen Points: *promote production*, but left out the first half of it: *grasp revolution*. The Municipal Party Committee would have nothing to do with the rebel workers' Headquarters. They would not even recognize it, let alone support it.

The Central Committee sent Chang Chun-chao, who had supported the Cultural Revolution from the beginning, to Shanghai to settle the question of the relation of the workers' Headquarters to the Party Committee. He asked Chen and

Chao to hold a meeting; they succeeded in encircling him and no good came of it. Meanwhile, however, the rebels were gaining strength. At the beginning of November, the rebel Headquarters had less than 10,000 members, by the end of the month, 500,000. The balance of forces was changing drastically. Consequently cadres in the municipality were taking courage to defy the Party leadership and stand up with the workers. The cadres in a number of offices of the municipality declared for the rebels at this time This was an explosion in the back yard of the enemy. (My informant belonged to this group. His eyes were opened by the October meeting of the Central Committee.) Cadres could play a particular role in the revolution that workers could not undertake. Students had been in the vanguard, but they did not know the Municipal Party Committee from the inside; workers know something of the Party Committee and they can transform public opinion, but only the cadres of the municipality know the detail of what is going on and understand the problems of organization. The adherence of the municipal cadres to the revolution made a great change in public opinion. The threefold revolutionary army of students, workers, and cadres was potentially a great force. If they united, the handful of reactionaries opposing them would collapse.

This was the end of the second part of stage two of the Cultural Revolution.

Desperation of the Rightists

The Mayor and First Secretary would not yet admit defeat. They encouraged the group of workers whom they had bamboozled to form a conservative organization to oppose the rebels under the title of the Red Militia Detachment. (No one, obviously, would consciously form a white organization.)

In December violent incidents broke out under the insti-
gation of Chen and Chao. At the same time they resorted to
more insidious methods. They stirred up the black wind of
'economism'. Pretending that the rebellion was due merely to
workers' grievances, they were extremely sympathetic. They
paid bonus wages, discovered arrears that were overdue,
offered full rates to apprentices. This created new conflicts
between young workers and the old hands. Everyone could
have whatever he asked for. Some workers who were put on to
a higher scale demanded ten years' back pay. Some individuals
pocketed two or three thousand yuan (a normal wage is
60 yuan per month). The reactionaries encouraged groups of
workers to go off to Peking to join the revolution. They quoted
Mao's 'grasp revolution' and forgot 'promote production'.
They paid travel allowances for the trip. Their slogan was
now 'hold tight on politics but relax on economics'. Workers
roamed around buying up goods and creating scarcities in the
market.

Some factories ceased production altogether. (Some
picturesque detail was supplied by the famous Wharf No. 5
which played a dramatic role in the revolution. A ship from
West Germany was berthed. It should have been unloaded
from four holds, but so many dockers were off on trips that
those who remained could only work on two. They were
falling badly behind schedule and the captain was abusing
them, saying the Cultural Revolution was nothing but a strike
and reviling the name of Mao Tse-tung. When the dockers
reported what was going on, they called back enough men to
put on a rush job and completed the work of four days in two,
four hours ahead of schedule. When the ship was getting off
the dockers shouted: You cannot abuse the Cultural Revolution. The captain cried in English: Yes, yes; the Chinese
workers are glorious under the leadership of Chairman Mao.

One young docker bought a watch with his 'economism'

money and proudly showed it to his father. His father, an old docker himself, told him that in the old days during a strike in which he was involved, the leader of thirty men was bought by the capitalist employer, with the result that many workers were imprisoned or sacked. The young man understood that the watch was handcuffing him. He rushed back, returned it to the shop, and threw the money at the feet of the man who had given it to him.

To create further confusion, the reactionaries got at some communes where former workers had been sent back to the country during the bad years, and told them that they had been wronged and should come into town again, thus leaving the commune short-handed. Finally they incited the Red Militia Detachment to cut off electricity, water and transport for the city, so as to create chaos, in order to put pressure on the Central Committee, saying: Look what your precious Cultural Revolution is coming to.

From the end of December till early January the situation was serious. The port, with a capacity for handling 80,000 tons a day was moving no more than 30,000 tons per day at the end of December. Foreign ships were queueing up in the river. Trains were immobilized on the tracks. (When the black wind of 'economism' was blowing, some workers captured a train to ride to Peking; rebel groups stopped it, so that the line was blocked for several days.) Only one or two trains a day were coming and going. Supplies in the city were falling.

Chang Chun-chao and Yao Wen-yuan visited Shanghai once more. In the discussion with them the workers said: Is it the Mayor and the Party Secretary who work on the docks and the railways? We can work them ourselves. Thus the rebels began to realize the necessity of seizing power. The seizure of power was a natural development of the Cultural Revolution. As long as the reactionaries were in official seats of authority and had the keys of the safe in their hands, the revolution could not be completed. The black wind of economism taught the workers this lesson. This was the end of the second stage of the Cultural Revolution in Shanghai.

The Seizure of Power

The third stage, which began in January 1967, was completed about the end of that year. All institutions and enterprises where reactionaries were still in positions of authority had to be taken over, and Revolutionary Representative Committees had to create temporary organs of power to administer them.

In the January Storm the conflict was very sharp. Every group and class had to stand and show itself. At least 700 different mass organizations were formed at the level of the municipality. Some belonged to genuine revolutionary groups, some were conservative, some wanted to take advantage of economism. A few were actually counter-revolutionaries. Each had its own motives and its own purposes. The struggle was extremely complicated.

The first move in seizing power was to capture the organs influencing public opinion. The chief daily newspapers of Shanghai were taken over by the rebels on 4 and 5 January. They could begin to make their own propaganda, in the same way as the reactionaries had begun their campaign in 1962 by working on public opinion.

Next they got control of the railways, the water and electricity supply, and the banks. They frustrated the scheme to disorganize the city and got services running. The old Municipal Party Committee and municipal government existed in form but were reduced to impotence. A great rally was called to dismiss the Mayor. He was informed that he was no longer recognized as Mayor. The business of municipal government was taken over by the Operational Headquarters of the rebellion. An Operational Headquarters was set up to combat economism and get the workers back to work. Meanwhile, the public was called in to help with the work at the docks and on the railways. Students and workers' groups sometimes worked twenty-four hours a day; one man for three days on end.

Leading rebel organizations posted up an 'Urgent Notice to the People of Shanghai'.* The appeal was to resist economism and rally to the rebel Headquarters.

Chairman Mao gave it his warm approval. He said it was the second Marxist-Leninist big character poster, because it raised the question of seizing power at the level of the whole city.

After converting public opinion and getting control over the economy of the city, the next step was to grasp power over the administration and over the Party. Chang and Yao argued that the various revolutionary groups must form a Great Alliance before assuming power. If some groups were excluded, disputes would break out and the new régime would be unstable. Actually power was taken and lost four times over. The first four times only a few organizations participated; on one occasion only two. Chang and Yao tried to persuade the rebel groups that a narrowly based seizure of power was useless, as the organs left out will then be hostile to the new régime. In Nanking, for example, this mistake was made. A few rebel groups joined together to form a temporary organ of power at the end of January. They were called the *Goods*, because they maintained it was good to take power. They were opposed by the *No goods* who held the contrary opinion. By November 1967 the situation in Nanking was satisfactory, but only after more than six months of internecine struggle between two sets of rebel groups. The moral was that a Great Alliance amongst the rebel groups must precede the seizure of power. In Shanghai, after four attempts, the lesson was learned and sufficient unity established to make the

*See p. 101.

seizure of power irreversible. At the fifth attempt, on 5 February, thirty-eight revolutionary organizations joined together; Chang and Yao themselves took part. The situation improved rapidly as a result of the Great Alliance in the fifth seizure of power. Chang and Yao were now working with the representatives of the rebel groups, which strengthened their committee and gave it prestige. To have cadres who have proved themselves good revolutionaries in alliance with the rebel groups is essential.

The Revolutionary Committee was formed, not without further struggles. The Committee had to eliminate on the one side followers of the capitalist road, the main target, and on the other, bad elements disguised as rebels. Some ex-landlords and rightists had insinuated themselves into the organization – it only needs twenty cents to buy a red armband – in order to carry out sabotage and create disorder. Some of the revolutionaries also, though good at heart, had fallen into error. The University Red Guards Revolutionary Committee, in particular, developed a mood of anarchism and 'down with everything'ism. They were suspicious even of Chang and Yao, crying: Down with them! This made it impossible to get the Committee set up. Revolutionary groups were organized to combat this irresponsibility. The Cultural Revolutionary Group of the Central Committee sent a telegram in support of them, which convinced the students of their mistake.

The Committee was then established. Formerly, the City Party Committee was a separate organization from the People's Council which comprised the administration of the municipality. Now Party and administration are integrated in the Revolutionary Committee.

The Committee is an alliance of three elements. First leading cadres; in the beginning only Chang and Yao were found worthy, but later some former members of the Shanghai Party Secretariat and some cadres were liberated and put into the Committee. (My informant was one of these.) Secondly, members of PLA units stationed in the area. (No individual soldier is kept for long spells on civilian duties.) And thirdly, representatives of the rebel groups which grew up spontaneously during the struggle.

In principle, half of the members of the Committee should be cadres from the old Municipal Party Committee, one quarter PLA and one quarter leaders of the mass organizations.

Former highly placed cadres are taking the lead in the new set up because of their knowledge and experience. Some of them had made mistakes and followed a reactionary line; through criticism from the workers, they recognize their mistakes and are forgiven by the rebels. In judging the worth of a cadre, it is wrong to look only at his behaviour during the struggle. His whole history must be taken into account. Most are judged as good. Their working style has been much improved (bossiness and secretiveness have been eliminated). Contact with the PLA has made a great change for the better. The leaders of the rebel organizations brought to the rest a fine fighting spirit. The Committee is different indeed from the old Party Committee and municipal government. The attitude of the public too has changed. They are guided by the Thought of Mao Tse-tung which teaches them to judge for themselves, not to follow authority blindly as they had in the past. If the Committee departs from Mao's line the masses will rise against them. The discarded reactionaries, who themselves operated bureaucratically, abuse them as bureaucrats. But on the contrary, they keep in touch with the masses and are their servants.

The first phase of the seizure of power and the setting up of the temporary organ of government lasted roughly from January till April. In April a new phase began – the criticism of China's Khrushchev, Liu Shao-ch'i.

Criticism and Repudiation

From April to September 1967 the Cultural Revolution passed through a phase of criticism of Liu Shao-ch'i and repudiation of his policies.

(For the Chinese public, Liu has ceased to be an individual human being; he is a symbol of the capitalist road. If he were thought of as a person, there would be an unpleasant streak of spitefulness in the caricatures of him and his wife that appear on many posters; but he is not; he is an effigy like Guy Fawkes. At the time – November 1967 – the actual man presumably was under some kind of house arrest. He had not been formally deprived of the office of President; nor had he been officially named, but the tiresome convention of referring to him only as 'the top Party person in authority taking the capitalist road' or as 'the Chinese Khrushchev' was breaking down in private conversation.)

The criticism of Liu was really a continuation of the seizure of power. We must not only seize power organizationally, that is simple. The real problem is to seize power politically and theoretically. It was easy to dismiss the Mayor and the Party Secretary. It is more complicated to take power politically and ideologically so as finally to discredit them.

It would be simple to dismiss Liu Shao-ch'i from office; the important thing is to overthrow the ideas that he stands for. Otherwise his like will come back some day.

In April started a period of systematic analysis and criticism of various aspects of what Liu stands for.

First of all, slavishness and blind obedience have had a great influence in the Party in China and all over the world. Party members were taught to follow their leader blindly without asking if a particular policy was correct or not. Some party members in other countries are nowadays criticizing slavishness.

T—c

A debate was still going on over the seizure of power. There was conflict over the question of the right and wrong way to take power. Can violence be avoided? The debate itself broke out into violence. In July and August 1967 there was actual fighting in Shanghai, at first with fists and then with guns. Transportation was disrupted by violence, and there was damage to production.

There is nothing strange about an outbreak of violence in a revolutionary situation. First, the Party persons taking the capitalist road succeeded in setting groups of workers against each other. There were examples of this in Shanghai. Secondly, some organizations which pretended to be on the side of the rebels were actually under the influence of ex-landlords, old rightists who had been thrown out in 1957, and so forth, who merely wanted to revenge themselves by making trouble. One of these groups had the insolence to propose their own list of candidates for the Revolutionary Committee and plotted to get themselves into power. Thirdly, there are still some wrong attitudes among the masses, such as factionalism and anarchism. Some wanted to seize power only for their own small group. In clashes between groups there was a loss of production and some disorder.

The Committee opposes violence. If it is correctly handled, violence may be a bad thing turned into a good thing – through violence, bad elements expose themselves, and the masses learn from their mistakes. Chairman Mao teaches us: 'We are not afraid of violence or disturbances. The greater the disturbance, the more contradictions can be exposed and the more easily can problems be solved.'

In August 1967, in Shanghai, there were several incidents of violence. Class lines became clearer. In September Chairman Mao (who visited Shanghai in secret on his tour of inspection, preparing for 1 October) called on the rebel groups to make a Great Alliance. (He proclaimed: 'There is no fundamental clash of interests within the working class. Under the dictatorship of the proletariat, there is no reason whatsoever for the working class to split into two big irreconcilable organizations.') In November, in the high tide of the Great Alliance, in places where disturbances were the greatest, the alliance is firmest. In Kiangsi, for instance, where there was fighting with guns, the situation is now excellent, in some ways even better than in Shanghai. In the coal mines of Hwai Nan, there was serious violence in July and August. Some mining installations were damaged. In September a Great Alliance was formed. Production had begun to recover. The mines were recently shown, at the Chairman's suggestion, to a distinguished visitor – the Prime Minister of the Congo (B).

During the worst period, July and August, Chairman Mao was not in Peking – he was visiting places where violence had broken out. His guards were very anxious for his safety; some begged him to stay in Peking; some tried to persuade him at least to travel by air, but he said that you see more from a train.

Economic Consequences

How was production in Shanghai affected? From January to April, after the Great Storm, it was increasing sharply. In May and June there were disturbances; the overall production remained at the level that had been reached in April. From January to June 1967 overall production was 3 per cent higher than in the same months in 1966. Throughout the disturbances of July and August, production was reduced in some enterprises. The worst difficulty was the shortage of coal due to the damage at the mines and the interference with transport. With the formation of the Great Alliance in September, industrial production rose. When the problem of coal has been settled, there will be a great upward bound in manufacturing. Already in many factories output is rising fast. The problem now to be considered is how to make the best use of greatly increased supplies. Output for January to October 1967 is about the same as for 1966. It is possible that for the whole year we shall have caught up, so that the total for 1967 will be no less than for 1966 and perhaps greater.

Agriculture was not adversely affected. The summer crop for 1967 was about 10 per cent higher than in 1966. The autumn crop was not yet all in in November; it is estimated to be 10 to 20 per cent higher than in 1966. Warehouses for the storage of autumn crops are being built.

The Next Phase

From 1 October 1967, a new situation developed. Following the directive to 'combat self interest and eradicate revisionism from our own minds,' the Cultural Revolution goes deeper. Everyone must accept a new orientation and remould his way of thinking to eliminate self interest. The Cultural Revolution cannot be consolidated without the remoulding of the ideology of all the people. If the seed of egoism is not eliminated, capitalism and revisionism may sprout again.

At present (in November 1967) the situation of the Cultural Revolution is not merely satisfactory but excellent. It is a rousing of the masses and participation by them in state affairs such as has never been seen in history before.

The debate goes on. Every family reunion falls into discussion of the Cultural Revolution. In every family there are differences of opinion to talk over. In one, the husband may be on one side, the wife on another and the mother-in-law on a third. In the country, every family is continuously hold-ing a meeting. The daughter may be the chairman; grandfather and mother take part in the argument. This was never known before in China.

Although we have an H-bomb, we believe that bombs are paper tigers – it is people who count.

Tasks Ahead

Many cadres have been criticized to great or less degree. The Cultural Revolution was primarily a movement to check up on cadres. The majority turned out to be in the first two categories outlined in the Sixteen Points – that is, good or fairly good. Many who made mistakes have turned back to Chairman Mao's line There is a very small number who are incorrigible. Even Chen and Chao could find a way out if they would correct their mistakes. There are still bourgeois elements with whom we can work, provided that they correct their attitude. Amongst the bourgeois intellectuals, only a handful of 'scholar tyrants' have to be thrown out. The general run of intellectuals will accept criticism from the masses. Even if they are bourgeois, they are not necessarily reactionaries. Chairman Mao's policy: 'Unite with those who can be united with' is the rule that we follow.

We expect that the seizure of power in all units in Shanghai will be completed by the end of 1967. Today (that is, in the middle of November 1967) there is already a Great Alliance in 90 per cent of Shanghai factories, and Revolutionary Committees in 60 to 70 per cent of them.

Great tasks remain to be undertaken – in particular education must be reorganized from top to bottom so that the next generation will not be a new set of bourgeois intellectuals but will be trained to serve the people and to keep in touch with the masses.

3
DOCUMENTS

1. The Circular of 16 May 1966

IN the course of the struggle the 'Cultural Revolution' came to have a wide meaning, affecting every aspect of life. In the early months of 1966 it had the restricted sense of an argument concerning the nature of art and literature in a socialist society. The Group of Five, appointed by the Central Committee to report on the issue, produced a document in February, which was repudiated by the Central Committee in the following circular issued on 16 May. The circular brought into the open a sharp political division within the Party; it allowed the public to know that the views and policies of Chairman Mao were being flouted by individuals in positions of the highest authority, and, in effect, it called upon the people to support him against them. As we were told in Shanghai, it was much later that the public in general realized that the 'top Party person' – Liu Shao-ch'i, the President of the Republic – was involved. At this stage, it was assumed that Peng Chen was the leader of Mao's opponents. This was quite sufficiently shocking, for he was known to be an influential member of the Political Bureau and he was Mayor of Peking. The clear and forceful language of the circular alerted Mao's supporters and encouraged an outburst of criticism, led by the famous poster protesting against the policies of the Principal of Peking University. It also, no doubt, alerted the Rightists to the fact that skirmishes in the field of culture were leading to a serious political conflict.

Some of the arguments attributed to bourgeois intellectuals, such as: 'Everyone is equal before the truth', still no doubt appeal to bourgeois intellectuals here. Unfortunately (like the old opera) they became discredited by the use to which they were put.

CIRCULAR OF THE CENTRAL COMMITTEE OF THE CHINESE COMMUNIST PARTY
(16 May 1966)

To all regional bureaux of the Central Committee, all provincial, municipal and autonomous region Party committees, all departments and commissions under the Central Committee, all leading Party members' groups and Party committees in government departments and people's organizations, and the General Political Department of the People's Liberation Army:

The Central Committee has decided to revoke the Outline Report on the Current Academic Discussion made by the Group of Five in Charge of the Cultural Revolution which was approved for distribution on 12 February 1966, to dissolve the 'Group of Five in Charge of the Cultural Revolution' and its offices, and to set up a new Cultural Revolution Group directly under the Standing Committee of the Political Bureau. The so-called Outline Report by the 'Group of Five' is fundamentally wrong. It runs counter to the line of the socialist cultural revolution set forth by the Central Committee and Comrade Mao Tse-tung and to the guiding principles formulated at the Tenth Plenary Session of the Eighth Central Committee of the Party in 1962 on the question of classes and class struggle in socialist society. While feigning compliance, the Report actually opposes and stubbornly resists the great cultural revolution personally initiated and led by Comrade Mao Tse-tung, as well as the instructions regarding the criticism of Wu Han which he gave at the Working Conference of the Central Committee in September and October of 1965 (that is, at the session of the Standing Committee of the Political Bureau of the Central Committee which was also attended by the leading comrades of all the regional bureaux of the Central Committee).

The so-called Outline Report by the 'Group of Five' is actually the Report of Peng Chen alone. He concocted it according to his own ideas behind the backs of Comrade Kang Sheng, a member of the 'Group of Five', and other comrades. In handling a document of this kind regarding important questions which affect the over-all situation in the socialist revolution, Peng Chen held no discussion or exchange of views at all within the 'Group of Five'. He did not ask any local Party committee for its opinion, nor did he make it clear that the Outline Report would be sent to the Central Committee for examination as an official document, and still less did he get the approval of Comrade Mao Tse-tung, Chairman of the Central Committee. Employing the most dishonest methods, he acted arbitrarily, abused his powers and, usurping the name of the Central Committee, hurriedly issued the Outline Report to the whole Party.

The main errors of the Outline Report are as follows:

1. Proceeding from a bourgeois stand and the bourgeois world outlook, the Report completely transposes the enemy and ourselves, putting the one into the position of the other, in its appraisal of the situation and the character of the present academic criticism. Our country is now in an upsurge of the Great Proletarian Cultural Revolution which is pounding at all the decadent ideological and cultural positions still held by the bourgeoisie and the remnants of feudalism. Instead of encouraging the entire Party boldly to arouse the broad masses of workers, peasants and soldiers and the fighters for proletarian culture so that they can continue to charge ahead, the Report does its best to turn the movement to the Right. Using muddled, self-contradictory and hypocritical language, it obscures the sharp class struggle that is taking place on the cultural and ideological front. In particular, it obscures the aim of this great struggle, which is to criticize and repudiate Wu Han and the considerable number of other anti-Party and anti-socialist representatives of the bourgeoisie (there are a number of them in the Central Committee and in Party, government and other departments at the central as well as at the provincial, municipal and autonomous region

levels). By avoiding any mention of the fact repeatedly pointed out by Chairman Mao, namely, that the heart of Wu Han's drama *Hai Jui Dismissed from Office* is the question of dismissal from office, the Report covers up the serious political nature of the struggle.

2. The Report violates the basic Marxist thesis that all class struggles are political struggles. When the press began to touch on the political issues involved in Wu Han's *Hai Jui Dismissed from Office*, the authors of the Report went so far as to say: 'The discussion in the press should not be confined to political questions, but should go fully into the various academic and theoretical questions involved.' Regarding the criticism of Wu Han, they declared on various occasions that it was impermissible to deal with the heart of the matter, namely, the dismissal of the Right opportunists at the Lushan Meeting in 1959 and the opposition of Wu Han and others to the Party and socialism. Comrade Mao Tse-tung has often told us that the ideological struggle against the bourgeoisie is a protracted class struggle which cannot be resolved by drawing hasty political conclusions. However, Peng Chen deliberately spread rumours, telling many people that Chairman Mao believed political conclusions on the criticism of Wu Han could be drawn after two months. Peng Chen also said that the political issues could be discussed two months later. His purpose was to channel the political struggle in the cultural sphere into so-called pure academic discussion, as frequently advocated by the bourgeoisie. Clearly, this means giving prominence to bourgeois politics, while opposing giving prominence to proletarian politics.

3. The Report lays special emphasis on what it calls 'opening wide'. But, playing a sly trick, it grossly distorts the policy of 'opening wide' expounded by Comrade Mao Tse-tung at the Party's National Conference on Propaganda Work in March 1957 and negates the class content of 'opening wide'. It was in dealing with this question that Comrade Mao Tse-tung pointed out: 'We still have to wage a protracted struggle against bourgeois

and petty-bourgeois ideology. It is wrong not to understand this and to give up ideological struggle. All erroneous ideas, all poisonous weeds, and all ghosts and monsters, must be subjected to criticism; in no circumstance should they be allowed to spread unchecked.' Comrade Mao Tse-tung also said: 'To "open wide" means to let all people express their opinions freely, so that they dare to speak, dare to criticize and dare to debate. . . .' This Report, however, poses 'opening wide' against the proletariat's exposure of the bourgeoisie's reactionary stand. What it means by 'opening wide' is bourgeois liberalization, which would allow only the bourgeoisie to 'open wide', but would not allow the proletariat to 'open wide' and hit back at the bourgeoisie; in other words, it is a shield for such reactionary representatives of the bourgeoisie as Wu Han. The 'opening wide' of this Report is opposed to Mao Tse-tung's thought and caters to the needs of the bourgeoisie.

4. Just when we began the counter-offensive against the wild attacks of the bourgeoisie, the authors of the Report raised the slogan: 'Everyone is equal before the truth.' This is a bourgeois slogan. Completely negating the class nature of truth, they use this slogan to protect the bourgeoisie and oppose the proletariat, oppose Marxism-Leninism and oppose Mao Tse-tung's thought. In the struggle between the proletariat and the bourgeoisie, between the truth of Marxism and the fallacies of the bourgeoisie and all other exploiting classes, either the East Wind prevails over the West Wind or the West Wind prevails over the East Wind, and there is absolutely no such thing as equality. Can equality be permitted on such basic questions as the struggle of the proletariat against the bourgeoisie, the dictatorship of the proletariat over the bourgeoisie, the dictatorship of the proletariat in the superstructure, including all the various spheres of culture, and the continued efforts of the proletariat to weed out those representatives of the bourgeoisie who have sneaked into the Communist Party and who wave 'red flags' to oppose the red flag? For decades the old-line Social Democrats, and for over ten years the modern revisionists, have never allowed the proletariat equal-

ity with the bourgeoisie. They completely deny that the several thousand years of human history are a history of class struggle. They completely deny the class struggle of the proletariat against the bourgeoisie, the proletarian revolution against the bourgeoisie and the dictatorship of the proletariat over the bourgeoisie. On the contrary, they are faithful lackeys of the bourgeoisie and the imperialists. Together with the bourgeoisie and the imperialists, they cling to the bourgeois ideology of oppression and exploitation of the proletariat and to the capitalist system, and they oppose Marxist-Leninist ideology and the socialist system. They are a bunch of counter-revolutionaries opposing the Communist Party and the people. Their struggle against us is one of life and death, and there is no question of equality. Therefore our struggle against them, too, can be nothing but a life-and-death struggle, and our relationship with them can in no way be one of equality. On the contrary, it is a relationship in which one class oppresses another, that is, the dictatorship of the proletariat over the bourgeoisie. There can be no other type of relationship, such as a so-called relationship of equality or of peaceful coexistence between exploiting and exploited classes, or of kindness or magnanimity.

5. The Report states: 'It is necessary not only to beat the other side politically, but also truly to surpass and beat it by a wide margin by academic and professional standards.' This concept which makes no class distinction on academic matters is also very wrong. The truth on academic questions, the truth of Marxism-Leninism, of Mao Tse-tung's thought – which the proletariat has grasped – has already far surpassed and beaten the bourgeoisie. The formulation in the Report shows that its authors laud the bourgeois academic so-called authorities and try to boost their prestige, and that they hate and repress the militant new forces representative of the proletariat in academic circles.

6. Chairman Mao often says that there is no construction without destruction. Destruction means criticism and repudiation, it

means revolution. It involves reasoning things out, which is construction. Put destruction first, and in the process you have construction. Marxism-Leninism, Mao Tse-tung's thought, was founded and has constantly developed in the course of the struggle to destroy bourgeois ideology. But this Report emphasizes that 'without construction, there can be no real and thorough destruction'. This amounts to prohibiting the destruction of bourgeois ideology and prohibiting the construction of proletarian ideology. It is diametrically opposed to Chairman Mao's thought. It runs counter to the revolutionary struggle we have been waging on the cultural front for the large-scale destruction of bourgeois ideology. And it amounts to prohibiting the proletariat from making any revolution.

7. The Report states that 'we must not behave like scholar-tyrants who always act arbitrarily and try to overwhelm people with their power' and that 'we should guard against any tendency by academic workers of the Left to take the road of bourgeois experts and scholar-tyrants'. What is really meant by 'scholar-tyrants'? Who are the 'scholar-tyrants'? Should the proletariat not exercise dictatorship and overwhelm the bourgeoisie? Should the academic work of the proletariat not overwhelm and eradicate that of the bourgeoisie? And if proletarian academic work overwhelms and eradicates bourgeois academic work, can this be regarded as an act of 'scholar-tyrants'? The Reports directs its spearhead against the proletarian Left. Obviously, its aim is to label the Marxist-Leninists 'scholar-tyrants' and thus to support the real, bourgeois scholar-tyrants and prop up their tottering monopoly position in academic circles. As a matter of fact, those Party people in authority taking the capitalist road who support the bourgeois scholar-tyrants and those bourgeois representatives who have sneaked into the Party and protect the bourgeois scholar-tyrants are big Party tyrants who have usurped the name of the Party. They do not read books, do not read the daily press, have no contact with the masses, have no learning at all, and rely solely on 'acting arbitrarily and trying to overwhelm people with their power'.

8. For their own ulterior purposes, the authors of the Report demand a 'rectification campaign' against the staunch Left in a deliberate effort to create confusion, blur class alignments and divert people from the target of struggle. Their main purpose in dishing up the Report in such a hurry was to attack the proletarian Left. They have gone out of their way to build up dossiers about the Left, tried to find all sorts of pretexts for attacking it, and intended to launch further attacks on it by means of a 'rectification campaign', in the vain hope of disintegrating its ranks. They openly resist the policy explicitly put forward by Chairman Mao of protecting and supporting the Left and giving serious attention to building it up and expanding its ranks. On the other hand, they have conferred the title of 'staunch Left' on those bourgeois representatives, revisionists and renegades who have sneaked into the Party and are shielding them. In these ways, they are trying to inflate the arrogance of the bourgeois Rightists and to dampen the spirits of the proletarian Left. They are filled with hatred for the proletariat and love for the bourgeoisie. Such is the bourgeois conception of brotherhood held by the authors of the Report.

9. At a time when the new and fierce struggle of the proletariat against the representatives of the bourgeoisie on the ideological front has only just begun – in many spheres and places it has not even started, or if it has started, most Party committees concerned have a very poor understanding of the task of leadership in this great struggle and their leadership is far from conscientious and effective – the Report stresses again and again that the struggle must be conducted 'under direction', 'with prudence', 'with caution', and 'with the approval of the leading bodies concerned'. All this serves to place restrictions on the proletarian Left, to impose taboos and commandments in order to tie its hands, and to place all sorts of obstacles in the way of the proletarian cultural revolution. In a word, the authors of the Report are rushing to apply the brakes and launch a vindictive counter-attack. As for the articles written by the proletarian Left in refuting the reactionary bourgeois 'authorities', they nurse bitter hatred against

those already published and are suppressing those not yet published. On the other hand they give free rein to all the ghosts and monsters who for many years have abounded in our press, radio, magazines, books, text-books, platforms, works of literature, cinema, drama, ballads and stories, the fine arts, music, the dance, etc., and in doing so they never advocate proletarian leadership or stress any need for approval. The contrast here shows where the authors of the Report really stand.

10. The present struggle centres around the issue of implementation of or resistance to Comrade Mao Tse-tung's line on the cultural revolution. Yet the Report states: 'Through this struggle, and under the guidance of Mao Tse-tung's thought, we shall open up the way for the solution of this problem [that is, "the thorough liquidation of bourgeois ideas in the realm of academic work"].' Comrade Mao Tse-tung opened up the way for the proletariat on the cultural and ideological front long ago, in his 'On New Democracy', 'Talks at the Yenan Forum on Literature and Art', 'Letter to the Yenan Peking Opera Theatre After Seeing *Driven to Join the Liangshan Mountain Rebels*', 'On the Correct Handling of Contradictions Among the People', and 'Speech at the Chinese Communist Party's National Conference on Propaganda Work'. Yet the Report maintains that Mao Tse-tung's thought has not yet opened up the way for us and that it has to be opened up anew. Using the banner of 'under the guidance of Mao Tse-tung's thought' as a cover, the Report actually attempts to open up a way opposed to Mao Tse-tung's thought, that is, the way of modern revisionism, the way to the restoration of capitalism.

In short, the Report opposes carrying the socialist revolution through to the end, opposes the line on the cultural revolution pursued by the Central Committee of the Party headed by Comrade Mao Tse-tung, attacks the proletarian Left and shields the bourgeois Right, thereby preparing public opinion for the restoration of capitalism. It is a reflection of bourgeois ideology in the Party; it is out-and-out revisionism. Far from being a minor issue, the struggle against this revisionist line is an issue of prime importance having a vital bearing on the destiny and future of our Party and state, on the future complexion of our Party and state, and on the world revolution.

Party committees at all levels must immediately stop carrying out the Outline Report on the Current Academic Discussion made by the Group of Five in Charge of the Cultural Revolution. The whole Party must follow Comrade Mao Tse-tung's instructions, hold high the great banner of the Proletarian Cultural Revolution, thoroughly expose the reactionary bourgeois stand of those so-called academic authorities who oppose the Party and socialism, thoroughly criticize and repudiate reactionary bourgeois ideas in the sphere of academic work, education, journalism, literature and art and publishing, and seize the leadership in these cultural spheres. To achieve this, it is at the same time necessary to criticize and repudiate those representatives of the bourgeoisie who have sneaked into the Party, the Government, the Army and all spheres of culture, and to clear them out or transfer some of them to other positions. Above all, we must not entrust these people with the work of leading the Cultural Revolution. In fact many of them have done and are still doing such work, and this is extremely dangerous.

Those representatives of the bourgeoisie who have sneaked into the Party, the Government, the Army and various spheres of culture are a bunch of counter-revolutionary revisionists. Once conditions are ripe, they will seize political power and turn the dictatorship of the proletariat into a dictatorship of the bourgeoisie. Some of them we have already seen through, others we have not. Some are still trusted by us and are being trained as our successors, persons like Khrushchev, for example, who are still nestling beside us. Party committees at all levels must pay full attention to this matter.

This Circular, together with the erroneous document issued by the Central Committee on 12 February 1966, is to be sent down to the level of county Party committees, Party committees in the cultural organizations and Party committees at regimental level in the Army. These committees are asked to discuss which of the two documents is wrong and which is correct, their understanding of these documents, and their achievements and mistakes.

2. Bombard the Headquarters

Chairman Mao returned to Peking at the end of July, 1966. A meeting of the Central Committee was summoned, which sat for ten days. Evidently there was a ferocious struggle between Mao and his supporters on the one side (who were at first in a minority) and the group led by Liu Shao-ch'i on the other. At this time the rebel students were hard pressed by the counter attacks of the Rightists, though small groups were keeping up the fight with posters and meetings.

In the midst of the argument Mao made the dramatic gesture of putting out a poster of his own.

BOMBARD THE HEADQUARTERS
MY BIG-CHARACTER POSTER
(5 August 1966)

MAO TSE-TUNG

China's first Marxist-Leninist big-character poster and Commentator's article on it in *Renmin Ribao* (People's Daily) are indeed superbly written! Comrades, please read them again. But in the last fifty days or so some leading comrades from the central down to the local levels have acted in a diametrically opposite way. Adopting the reactionary stand of the bourgeoisie, they have enforced a bourgeois dictatorship and struck down the surging movement of the Great Cultural Revolution of the proletariat. They have stood facts on their head and juggled black and white, encircled and suppressed revolutionaries, stifled opinions differing from their own, imposed a white terror, and felt very pleased with themselves. They have puffed up the arrogance of the bourgeoisie and deflated the morale of the proletariat. How poisonous! Viewed in connexion with the Right deviation in

1. A scene from *Taking the Bandits' Stronghold*, a contemporary revolutionary Peking opera (Hsinhua News Agency)

2. Red Guards and members of Peking University putting up 'big-character' posters (Hsinhua News Agency)

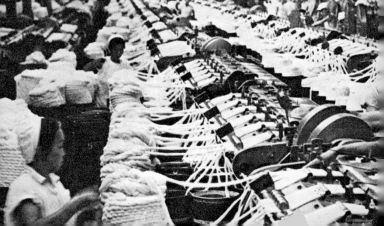

一个五年計划而

3. (*Top*) Mao meets teachers and students

4. (*Bottom*) Proletarian revolutionaries in a cotton mill in Tsingtao (both Hsinhua News Agency)

5. (*Top*) *Tachai*: Houses that escaped the flood

6. (*Bottom*) *Tachai*: Cutting stone to terrace the fields

7. (*Top*) The new Tachai begins to prosper

8. (*Bottom*) The threshing-ground of Tachai (both Hsinhua News Agency)

9. (*Top*) Marketing and
Supply Staff set out
for hill villages in
Tsai Ke Da, Shansi

10. (*Bottom*) Grinding
meal. A motor now
works the old stone
hand mill

1962 and the wrong tendency of 1964 which was 'Left' in form but Right in essence, shouldn't this make one wide awake?*

The 'first Marxist-Leninist big-character poster' to which Mao refers was the protest, now famous, against the President of Peking University, put up on 25 May 1966, by Nieh Yuan-tzu and other members of the Department of Philosophy. It was published in the press on 2 June. The commentator's article in the *People's Daily*† backs up the writers of the poster, heaps abuse on their enemies, and ends with: 'The revolutionary struggle of the great mass of teachers and students at Peking University opposing the representatives of the bourgeoisie are certain to emerge victorious. A new, flourishing and genuinely socialist Peking University is certain to emerge very soon in the people's capital.'

The first round had been won by the rebels. In June 1966, the Peking Party Committee had been reorganized and the President of Peking University dismissed, but the Rightists had recovered from this setback and seemed to be gaining ground. By putting up his poster, Mao was using the magic of his name to rally the students and the people against them.

'The Right deviation in 1962' refers to the period when the three bad years of harvest failures were over, but Liu Shao-ch'i was taking advantage of that experience to press for the economic ideas that he believed in, particularly the development of individualistic monetary incentives in agricultural production at the expense of the principles of cooperation and collective responsibility that Mao upheld. Liu advocated the extension of plots for private use, the extension of the rural

* The English translation was published in *Peking Review*, 1967, No. 33, on the anniversary of the appearance of the poster.

† An English translation was published in *Peking Review*, 1966, No. 37.

fairs at which individual households could sell their products
in conditions of a free market, the increase in the number of
small enterprises in the villages run on the principle of private
profit, and the fixing of output quotas in the annual production
plan on the basis of households instead of on the basis of teams
or brigades.*

The Socialist education campaign of 1963 and 1964 was
launched to 'clean up the four questions' of politics, ideology,
organization and the economy. Cadres were sent into the
countryside to get acquainted with local problems, smell out
defects in Party work and combat the 'spontaneous development of capitalism' which is a chronic temptation in a peasant
community.

The 'wrong tendency of 1964 which was "Left" in form but
Right in essence' in the poster is an allusion to the fact that
in some places the movement of 'four clean-ups' was captured
by Rightists (in this Liu's wife played an important part) so
that, under cover of Mao's phrases the 'capitalist road' was
being advocated.†

An episode such as the publication of Chairman Mao's own
poster has no analogue in Parliamentary terms. Mao Tse-tung
in one sense represented the opposition at this time, and Liu
the government. He had evidently been in a weak position
during the bad years that followed the Great Leap of 1958.
It was officially admitted that the disastrous harvest failures
were not only due to the formidable weather conditions of
those years but were partly due to mistakes in the Party's
work – political mistakes, such as forcing the pace in setting
up the communes, and technical mistakes such as the indis-
criminate application of rules, for instance, deep ploughing
and close planting, without considering the variations in local

* See *Peking Review*, 1967, No. 49, p. 15.
† ibid p. 17.

conditions. Mao's adversaries played up the mistakes. At this time the Rightists 'came to their high tide'.*

From 1962 onwards harvests improved, the shock of the withdrawal of the Soviet technicians was being overcome. (In 1964 it was being called a 'bad thing turned into a good thing' because it had stimulated Chinese technicians to crack the problems left unsolved, and their methods were better adapted to China's needs.) It may be supposed that the Chairman's position in the councils of the Party was growing stronger. The campaign for the 'four clean-ups' was in some places deflected to the purposes of the Rightists. In January 1965 Chairman Mao tried to get it back on to his line by issuing the directives known as the '23 article document'. In this he stated that the main target of the present movement is the Party persons in authority who are taking the capitalist road.† In September 1965 at a meeting of the Standing Committee of the Political Bureau of the Central Committee he threw out the challenge: 'What are you going to do if revisionism appears in the Central Committee? This is highly likely. This is the greatest danger.'‡

At that time, the conflict within the Central Committee which came into the open with the publication of the 16 May Circular in 1966 was growing sharper. No doubt it dates back to 1960, or perhaps to the Twentieth Congress in the Soviet Union in 1956.

It has something in common with an attack by a Parliamentary opposition upon the government in power. But the analogy is not close. To the people at large Mao *was* the government, although he had formally yielded the position of President to Liu Shao-ch'i and was nominally only Chairman of the Central Committee of the Communist Party of China. Moreover Mao, ever since Lin Piao was installed as

*Cf. p. 47.   †*Peking Review*, 1967, No. 33, p. 7.
‡ibid.

Minister of Defence in 1959, had been building up his influence in the PLA. His position cannot be equated to that of the Leader of the Opposition in the House of Commons.

Perhaps a better analogy would be the appeal of President Roosevelt to the American public in the period of the New Deal, over the heads of a recalcitrant Congress. But no analogy goes very far. In any case, this kind of formalistic approach to politics is alien to the Chinese tradition, which has always put Justice above Law.

3. The Sixteen Points

The Sixteen Points laid down the main lines that the Cultural Revolution was to follow, leaving, however, a great deal of play to spontaneous movement from below.

The document operates on a triple time span. It is concerned with the immediate situation, with developments over the next year or so and with long vistas of future improvement.

The first four sections and the seventh deal mainly with the situation when the document was first issued. At that time the rebels had to be encouraged and defended from the counter-attacks of the Rightists. Other portions, such as Sections 5, 8, 9, 14, and 16, deal with more general principles and give guidance for the development of the movement.

Section 10, on educational reform, deals with a long-term programme which will take years to complete.

Section 11 accounts for the habit of referring to Liu Shao-ch'i (the President), in all official pronouncements, as the Chinese Khrushchev, or the top Party person in authority taking the capitalist road, and Teng Hsiao-ping (the First Secretary of the Party) as the other top Party person, etc., while Ministers such as Po I-po and Tau Chu, who have been dismissed from their posts, are freely named by their names.

Section 13 deals with the movement generally known as the 'four clean-ups'. The directive of January 1965* was intended to get it back on to the rails where it had been deflected by the Rightists, and it was now to be merged with the Cultural Revolution.

DECISION OF
THE CENTRAL COMMITTEE OF
THE CHINESE COMMUNIST PARTY
CONCERNING THE
GREAT PROLETARIAN
CULTURAL REVOLUTION

(Adopted 8 August 1966)

1. A New Stage in the Socialist Revolution

The Great Proletarian Cultural Revolution now unfolding is a great revolution that touches people to their very souls and constitutes a new stage in the development of the socialist revolution in our country, a stage which is both broader and deeper.

At the Tenth Plenary Session of the Eighth Central Committee of the Party, Comrade Mao Tse-tung said: To overthrow a political power, it is always necessary first of all to create public opinion, to do work in the ideological sphere. This is true for the revolutionary class as well as for the counter-revolutionary class. This thesis of Comrade Mao Tse-tung's has been proved entirely correct in practice.

Although the bourgeoisie has been overthrown, it is still trying to use the old ideas, culture, customs and habits of the exploiting classes to corrupt the masses, capture their minds and endeavour to stage a come-back. The proletariat must do the exact opposite: it must meet head-on every challenge of the bourgeoisie in the ideological field and use the new ideas, culture, customs and habits of the proletariat to change the mental outlook of the whole of society. At present, our objective is to struggle against and overthrow those persons in authority who are taking the

* See above p. 82.

capitalist road, to criticize and repudiate the reactionary bourgeois academic 'authorities' and the ideology of the bourgeoisie and all other exploiting classes and to transform education, literature and art and all other parts of the superstructure not in correspondence with the socialist economic base, so as to facilitate the consolidation and development of the socialist system.

2. The main current and the twists and turns

The masses of the workers, peasants, soldiers, revolutionary intellectuals and revolutionary cadres form the main force in this great Cultural Revolution. Large numbers of revolutionary young people, previously unknown, have become courageous and daring pathbreakers. They are vigorous in action and intelligent. Through the media of big-character posters and great debates, they argue things out, expose and criticize thoroughly, and launch resolute attacks on the open and hidden representatives of the bourgeoisie. In such a great revolutionary movement, it is hardly avoidable that they should show shortcomings of one kind or another; however, their general revolutionary orientation has been correct from the beginning. This is the main current in the Great Proletarian Cultural Revolution. It is the general direction along which this revolution continues to advance.

Since the Cultural Revolution is a revolution, it inevitably meets with resistance. This resistance comes chiefly from those in authority who have wormed their way into the Party and are taking the capitalist road. It also comes from the force of habits from the old society. At present, this resistance is still fairly strong and stubborn. But after all, the Great Proletarian Cultural Revolution is an irresistible general trend. There is abundant evidence that such resistance will be quickly broken down once the masses become fully aroused.

Because the resistance is fairly strong, there will be reversals and even repeated reversals in this struggle. There is no harm in this. It tempers the proletariat and other working people, and especially the younger generation, teaches them lessons and gives them experience, and helps them to understand that the revolutionary road zigzags and does not run smoothly.

3. Put daring above everything else and boldly arouse the masses

The outcome of this great Cultural Revolution will be determined by whether or not the Party leadership dares boldly to arouse the masses.

Currently, there are four different situations with regard to the leadership being given to the movement of Cultural Revolution by Party organizations at various levels:

(i) There is the situation in which the persons in charge of Party organizations stand in the van of the movement and dare to arouse the masses boldly. They put daring above everything else, they are dauntless Communist fighters and good pupils of Chairman Mao. They advocate the big-character posters and great debates. They encourage the masses to expose every kind of ghost and monster and also to criticize the shortcomings and errors in the work of the persons in charge. This correct kind of leadership is the result of putting proletarian politics in the forefront and Mao Tse-tung's Thought in the lead.

(ii) In many units, the persons in charge have a very poor understanding of the task of leadership in this great struggle, their leadership is far from being conscientious and effective, and they accordingly find themselves incompetent and in a weak position. They put fear above everything else, stick to outmoded ways and regulations, and are unwilling to break away from conventional practices and move ahead. They have been taken unawares by the new order of things, the revolutionary order of the masses, with the result that their leadership lags behind the situation, lags behind the masses.

(iii) In some units, the persons in charge, who made mistakes of one kind or another in the past, are even more prone to put fear above everything else, being afraid that the masses will catch them out. Actually, if they make serious self-criticism and accept the criticism of the masses, the Party and the masses will make allowances for their mistakes. But if the persons in charge don't, they will continue to make mistakes and become obstacles to the mass movement.

(iv) Some units are controlled by those who have wormed their way into the Party and are taking the capitalist road. Such persons in authority are extremely afraid of being exposed by the masses and therefore seek every possible pretext to suppress the mass movement. They resort to such tactics as shifting the targets for attack and turning black into white in an attempt to lead the movement astray. When they find themselves very isolated and no longer able to carry on as before, they resort still more to intrigues, stabbing people in the back, spreading rumours, and blurring the distinction between revolution and counter-revolution as much as they can, all for the purpose of attacking the revolutionaries.

What the Central Committee of the Party demands of the Party committees at all levels is that they persevere in giving correct leadership, put daring above everything else, boldly arouse the masses, change the state of weakness and incompetence where it exists, encourage those comrades who have made mistakes but are willing to correct them to cast off their mental burdens and join in the struggle, and dismiss from their leading posts all those in authority who are taking the capitalist road and so make possible the recapture of the leadership for the proletarian revolutionaries.

4. Let the masses educate themselves in the movement

In the Great Proletarian Cultural Revolution, the only method is for the masses to liberate themselves, and any method of doing things in their stead must not be used.

Trust the masses, rely on them and respect their initiative. Cast out fear. Don't be afraid of disturbances. Chairman Mao has often told us that revolution cannot be so very refined, so gentle, so temperate, kind, courteous, restrained and magnanimous. Let the masses educate themselves in this great revolutionary movement and learn to distinguish between right and wrong and between correct and incorrect ways of doing things.

Make the fullest use of big-character posters and great debates to argue matters out, so that the masses can clarify the correct views, criticize the wrong views and expose all the ghosts and monsters. In this way the masses will be able to raise their political consciousness in the course of the struggle, enhance their abilities and talents, distinguish right from wrong and draw a clear line between ourselves and the enemy.

5. Firmly apply the class line of the Party

Who are our enemies? Who are our friends? This is a question of the first importance for the revolution and it is likewise a question of the first importance for the great Cultural Revolution.

Party leadership should be good at discovering the Left and developing and strengthening the ranks of the Left; it should firmly rely on the revolutionary Left. During the movement that is the only way to isolate the most reactionary Rightists thoroughly, win over the middle and unite with the great majority so that by the end of the movement we shall achieve the unity of more than 95 per cent of the cadres and more than 95 per cent of the masses.

Concentrate all forces to strike at the handful of ultra-reactionary bourgeois Rightists and counter-revolutionary revisionists, and expose and criticize to the full their crimes against the Party, against socialism and against Mao Tse-tung's thought so as to isolate them to the maximum.

The main target of the present movement is those within the Party who are in authority and are taking the capitalist road.

The strictest care should be taken to distinguish between the anti-Party, anti-socialist Rightists, and those who support the Party and socialism but have said or done something wrong or have written some bad articles or other works.

The strictest care should be taken to distinguish between the reactionary bourgeois scholar despots and 'authorities' on the one hand and people who have the ordinary bourgeois academic ideas on the other.

6. Correctly handle contradictions among the people

A strict distinction must be made between the two different types of contradictions: those among the people and those between ourselves and the enemy. Contradictions among the people must not be made into contradictions between ourselves and the enemy; nor must contradictions between ourselves and the enemy be regarded as contradictions among the people.

It is normal for the masses to hold different views. Contention between different views is unavoidable, necessary and beneficial. In the course of normal and full debate, the masses will affirm what is right, correct what is wrong and gradually reach unanimity.

The method to be used in debates is to present the facts, reason things out, and persuade through reasoning. Any method of forcing a minority holding different views to submit is impermissible. The minority should be protected, because sometimes the truth is with the minority. Even if the minority is wrong, they should still be allowed to argue their case and reserve their views.

When there is a debate, it should be conducted by reasoning, not by coercion or force.

In the course of debate, every revolutionary should be good at thinking things out for himself and should develop the communist spirit of daring to think, daring to speak and daring to act. On the premise that they have the same general orientation, revolutionary comrades should, for the sake of strengthening unity, avoid endless debate over side issues.

7. *Be on guard against those who brand the revolutionary masses as 'counter-revolutionaries'.*

In certain schools, units, and work teams of the Cultural Revolution, some of the persons in charge have organized counterattacks against the masses who put up big-character posters criticizing them. These people have even advanced such slogans as: Opposition to the leaders of a unit or a work team means opposition to the Central Committee of the Party, means opposition to the Party and socialism, means counter-revolution. In this way it is inevitable that their blows will fall on some really revolutionary activists. This is an error in matters of orientation, an error of line, and is absolutely impermissible.

A number of persons who suffer from serious ideological errors, and particularly some of the anti-Party and anti-socialist Rightists, are taking advantage of certain shortcomings and mistakes in the mass movement to spread rumours and gossip, and engage in agitation, deliberately branding some of the masses as 'counter-revolutionaries'. It is necessary to beware of such 'pick-pockets' and expose their tricks in good time.

In the course of the movement, with the exception of cases of active counter-revolutionaries where there is clear evidence of crimes such as murder, arson, poisoning, sabotage or theft of state secrets, which should be handled in accordance with the law, no measures should be taken against students at universities, colleges, middle schools and primary schools because of problems that arise in the movement. To prevent the struggle from being diverted from its main target, it is not allowed, under whatever pretext, to incite the masses or the students to struggle against each other. Even proven Rightists should be dealt with on the merits of each case at a later stage of the movement.

8. The question of cadres

The cadres fall roughly into the following four categories:

  (i) good;
  (ii) comparatively good;
  (iii) those who have made serious mistakes but have not become anti-Party, anti-socialist Rightists;
  (iv) the small number of anti-Party, anti-socialist Rightists.

In ordinary situations, the first two categories (good and comparatively good) are the great majority.

The anti-Party, anti-socialist Rightists must be fully exposed, refuted, overthrown and completely discredited and their influence eliminated. At the same time, they should be given a chance to turn over a new leaf.

9. Cultural revolutionary groups, committees and congresses

Many new things have begun to emerge in the Great Proletarian Cultural Revolution. The cultural revolutionary groups, committees and other organizational forms created by the masses in many schools and units are something new and of great historic importance.

These cultural revolutionary groups, committees and congresses are excellent new forms of organization whereby the masses educate themselves under the leadership of the Communist Party. They are an excellent bridge to keep our Party in close contact with the masses. They are organs of power of the Proletarian Cultural Revolution.

The struggle of the proletariat against the old ideas, culture, customs and habits left over by all the exploiting classes over thousands of years will necessarily take a very, very long time. Therefore, the cultural revolutionary groups, committees and congresses should not be temporary organizations but permanent, standing mass organizations. They are suitable not only for colleges, schools and government and other organizations, but generally also for factories, mines, other enterprises, urban districts and villages.

It is necessary to institute a system of general elections, like that of the Paris Commune, for electing members to the cultural revolutionary congresses. The lists of candidates should be put forward by the revolutionary masses after full discussion, and the elections should be held after the masses have discussed the lists over and over again.

The masses are entitled at any time to criticize members of the cultural revolutionary groups and committees and delegates elected to the cultural revolutionary congresses. If these members or delegates prove incompetent, they can be replaced through election or recalled by the masses after discussion.

The cultural revolutionary groups, committees and congresses in colleges and schools should consist mainly of representatives of the revolutionary students. At the same time, they should have a certain number of representatives of the revolutionary teaching and administrative staff and workers.

10. Educational reform

In the Great Proletarian Cultural Revolution a most important task is to transform the old educational system and the old principles and methods of teaching.

In this great Cultural Revolution, the phenomenon of our schools being dominated by bourgeois intellectuals must be completely changed.

In every kind of school we must apply thoroughly the policy advanced by Comrade Mao Tse-tung of education serving proletarian politics and education being combined with productive labour, so as to enable those receiving an education to develop morally, intellectually and physically and to become labourers with socialist consciousness and culture.

The period of schooling should be shortened. Courses should be fewer and better. The teaching material should be thoroughly transformed, in some cases beginning with simplifying complicated material. While their main task is to study, students should also learn other things. That is to say, in addition to their studies they should also learn industrial work, farming and military affairs, and take part in the struggles of the Cultural Revolution to criticize the bourgeoisie as these struggles occur.

11. The question of criticizing by name in the press

In the course of the mass movement of the Cultural Revolution, the criticism of bourgeois and feudal ideology should be well combined with the dissemination of the proletarian world outlook and of Marxism-Leninism, Mao Tse-tung's thought.

Criticism should be organized of typical bourgeois representatives who have wormed their way into the Party and typical reactionary bourgeois academic 'authorities', and this should include criticism of various kinds of reactionary views in philosophy, history, political economy and education, in works and theories of literature and art, in theories of natural science, and in other fields.

Criticism of anyone by name in the Press should be decided after discussion by the Party committee at the same level, and in some cases submitted to the Party committee at a higher level for approval.

12. Policy towards scientists, technicians and ordinary members of working staffs

As regards scientists, technicians and ordinary members of working staffs, as long as they are patriotic, work energetically, are not against the Party and socialism, and maintain no illicit relations with any foreign country, we should in the present movement continue to apply the policy of 'unity, criticism, unity'. Special care should be taken of those scientists and scientific and technical personnel who have made contributions. Efforts should be made to help them gradually transform their world outlook and their style of work.

13. The question of arrangements for integration with the socialist education movement in city and countryside

The cultural and educational units and leading organs of the Party and Government in the large and medium cities are the points of concentration of the present Proletarian Cultural Revolution.

The Great Cultural Revolution has enriched the socialist education movement in both city and countryside and raised it to a higher level. Efforts should be made to conduct these two movements in close combination. Arrangements to this effect may be made by various regions and departments in the light of the specific conditions.

The socialist education movement now going on in the countryside and in enterprises in the cities should not be upset where the original arrangements are appropriate and the movement is going well, but should continue in accordance with the original arrangements. However, the questions that are arising in the present Great Proletarian Cultural Revolution should be put to the masses for discussion at the proper time, so as to further foster vigorously proletarian ideology and eradicate bourgeois ideology.

In some places, the Great Proletarian Cultural Revolution is being used as the focus in order to add momentum to the socialist education movement and clean things up in the fields of politics, ideology, organization and economy. This may be done where the local Party committee thinks it appropriate.

14. Take firm hold of the Revolution and stimulate production

The aim of the Great Proletarian Cultural Revolution is to revolutionize people's ideology and as a consequence to achieve greater, faster, better and more economical results in all fields of work. If the masses are fully aroused and proper arrangements are made, it is possible to carry on both the Cultural Revolution and production without one hampering the other, while guaranteeing high quality in all our work.

The Great Proletarian Cultural Revolution is a powerful motive force for the development of the social productive forces in our country. Any idea of counterposing the Great Cultural Revolution to the development of production is incorrect.

15. The armed forces

In the armed forces, the Cultural Revolution and the socialist education movement should be carried out in accordance with the instructions of the Military Commission of the Central Committee of the Party and the General Political Department of the People's Liberation Army.

16. Mao Tse-tung's Thought is the guide to action in the Great Proletarian Cultural Revolution

In the Great Proletarian Cultural Revolution, it is imperative to hold aloft the great red banner of Mao Tse-tung's thought and put proletarian politics in command. The movement for the creative study and application of Chairman Mao Tse-tung's works should be carried forward among the masses of the workers, peasants and soldiers, the cadres and the intellectuals, and Mao Tse-tung's thought should be taken as the guide to action in the Cultural Revolution.

In this complex great Cultural Revolution, Party committees at all levels must study and apply Chairman Mao's works all the more conscientiously and in a creative way. In particular, they must study over and over again Chairman Mao's writings on the Cultural Revolution and on the Party's methods of leadership, such as 'On New Democracy', 'Talks at the Yenan Forum on Literature and Art', 'On the Correct Handling of Contradictions Among the People,' 'Speech at the Chinese Communist Party's National Conference on Propaganda Work,' 'Some Questions Concerning Methods of Leadership' and 'Methods of Work of Party Committees'.

Party committees at all levels must abide by the directions given by Chairman Mao over the years, namely that they should thoroughly apply the mass line of 'from the masses, to the masses' and that they should be pupils before they become teachers. They should try to avoid being one-sided or narrow. They should foster materialist dialectics and oppose metaphysics and scholasticism.

The Great Proletarian Cultural Revolution is bound to achieve brilliant victory under the leadership of the Central Committee of the Party headed by Comrade Mao Tse-tung.

4. The January Storm in Shanghai

The following documents illustrate the narrative of the capture of power in Shanghai.

The newspaper offices were seized by the Rebel Headquarters on 4 and 5 January. The following 'Message to the People of Shanghai' was immediately put out. On 9 January followed the famous 'Urgent Notice'. On 11 January this declaration was endorsed by a telegram from the Central Committee.

MESSAGE TO ALL SHANGHAI PEOPLE

Under the guidance of the proletarian revolutionary line represented by Chairman Mao, the Great Proletarian Cultural Revolution has won tremendous victories in the mass movement over the last few months in the criticism of the bourgeois reactionary line. We have entered the year 1967 to the sound of militant songs of triumph. It was pointed out in the New Year's Day editorial of *Renmin Ribao* and the journal *Hongqi*:

1967 will be a year of all-round development of class struggle throughout China. It will be a year in which the proletariat, united with other sections of the revolutionary masses, will launch a general attack on the handful of Party persons in authority who are taking the capitalist road, and on the ghosts and monsters in society. It will be a year of even more penetrating criticism and repudiation of the bourgeois reactionary line and elimination of its influence. It will be a year of decisive victory in carrying out the struggle [to overthrow those in authority who are taking the capitalist road], the criticism and repudiation [of the reactionary bourgeois academic 'authorities' and the ideology of the bourgeoisie and all other exploiting classes] and the transformation [of education, literature and art and all other parts of the superstructure not in correspondence with the socialist economic base].

In other words, it will be a year in which the bourgeois reactionary line will totally collapse and disintegrate completely, a year in which the Great Proletarian Cultural Revolution will win a great, decisive victory.

The broad revolutionary masses of Shanghai have also won an initial victory in the struggle to criticize and repudiate the bourgeois reactionary line implemented by a handful of people within the Party in Shanghai area and have carried the struggle to a deeper and broader new stage.

The mass movement of the Great Proletarian Cultural Revolution in our Shanghai factories is surging forward vigorously, smashing through all resistance with the might of an avalanche and the force of a thunderbolt. We, workers of the revolutionary rebel groups, follow Chairman Mao's teachings most closely and resolutely carried out the policy of 'taking firm hold of the revolution and promoting production' advanced by Chairman Mao himself. Chairman Mao teaches us: 'Political work is the life-blood of all economic work.'* We of the

* Quotation from the introductory note to 'A Serious Lesson', *The Socialist Upsurge in China's Countryside*.

T – D

revolutionary rebel groups clearly understand that if the Great Proletarian Cultural Revolution is not carried out well, we will lose our orientation in production and slide back in the direction of capitalism.

What we ourselves have experienced in the course of the Great Proletarian Cultural Revolution has increasingly proved to us that only if the Great Proletarian Cultural Revolution is carried out well, will production develop on a still greater scale. Any idea of counterposing the Great Cultural Revolution to the development of production is erroneous.

However, a handful of Party persons in authority who are taking the capitalist road and those who obstinately adhere to the bourgeois reactionary line have a bitter hatred for the Great Proletarian Cultural Revolution. They have been trying by every means to resist the policy of 'taking firm hold of the revolution and promoting production' put forward by Chairman Mao. Their schemes and devices may be summarized in the following ways:

At the beginning of the movement, they used the pretext of 'taking firm hold of production' to repress the revolution and oppose taking firm hold of the revolution. When we workers of the revolutionary rebel groups wanted to rise up in revolution and criticize and repudiate the bourgeois reactionary line, they used the tasks of production to bring pressure to bear on the workers and tagged us with the label of 'sabotaging production'. Did they really want to 'take firm hold of production'? No, they wanted to defend their own positions and attempted to obstruct our revolution. We exposed their schemes and rose up bravely in rebellion.

Then they resorted to another trick, that is, they played with high-sounding revolutionary words, giving the appearance of being exceedingly 'Left' in order to incite large numbers of members of the Workers' Red Militia Detachments whom they have hoodwinked to undermine production and sabotage transport and communications under the pretext of going north to 'lodge complaints'. They did this to attain their aim of undermining the Great Proletarian Revolution and the dictatorship of the proletariat. More recently, a handful of reactionary elements were even plotting to cut off water and electricity supplies and bring public transport to a standstill. We must drag out these reactionary elements and exercise proletarian dictatorship over them, punish them severely and never allow them to succeed in their criminal schemes.

Comrade revolutionary workers! Go into action at once! Resolutely carry out the policy of 'taking firm hold of the revolution and promoting production' advanced by Chairman Mao! We, workers of the revolutionary rebel groups, must become models in 'taking firm hold of the revolution and promoting production'. We must serve as the vanguards and the backbone not only in taking firm hold of the revolution, but also in promoting production. Our city of Shanghai, China's biggest industrial producer, plays an extremely important role in the overall economic life of the country. But lately, in many factories and plants, it has occurred that some or even the majority of the members of the Workers' Red Militia Detachments have suspended production and deserted their posts in production. This runs directly counter to the stipulation by the Party Central Committee on taking firm hold of the revolution and promoting production and directly affects the people's livelihood and the development of national economic construction. Our revolutionary rebel workers, bearing in mind the teachings of Chairman Mao, have stood our ground in the face of this adverse current, have given proof of our high sense of revolutionary responsibility and, under extremely difficult conditions, have shouldered all the production tasks of our factories and plants, thus dealing a telling blow against the handful of Party persons in authority who are taking the capitalist road, and smashing their big plot by which they attempted to thwart the revolution through sabotaging production. The actions of these workers are correct and splendid! All of us comrades of the revolutionary rebel groups should learn from them. Chairman Mao teaches us: 'We should support whatever the enemy opposes and oppose whatever the enemy supports.'* We, workers of the revolutionary rebel

*Mao Tse-tung, 'Interview with Three Correspondents from the Central News Agency, the *Sao Tang Pao* and the *Hsin Min Pao*',

groups, have the lofty aspiration, the determination and the strength to do still better in both revolution and production and to carry out Chairman Mao's great call for 'taking firm hold of the revolution and promoting production'.

The broad sections of our class brothers of the Workers' Red Militia Detachments who want to make revolution! 'Taking firm hold of the revolution and promoting production' is a policy put forward by Chairman Mao, a policy stressed time and again by the Party Central Committee, an important policy which guarantees the carrying through to the end of the Great Proletarian Cultural Revolution. To support or not to support, to carry out or not to carry out this policy is itself a matter of principle, a cardinal issue of right and wrong. In allowing yourselves to be incited by those people [Party persons in authority who are taking the capitalist road – *Tr.*] and by deserting your posts in production, whose interests are you serving? By acting in this way, whose hearts, after all, are you gladdening and whose are you saddening? We hope that you will follow Chairman Mao's teachings, that, on this important question of principle, you will see things more clearly, make a clear distinction between right and wrong, stop being deceived, wake up quickly, return to your posts in production and return to the proletarian revolutionary line. We, comrades of the revolutionary rebel groups, will certainly warmly welcome you back to make revolution along with us and improve production with us. We will certainly not blame you, because we are all close class brothers, and because the overwhelming majority of you are victims of the bourgeois reactionary line, are revolutionary masses who have been hood-winked by those within the Party who are in authority and taking the capitalist road and by those who are stubbornly following the bourgeois reactionary line.

All revolutionary students and revolutionary government cadres of the city! Let us closely unite with the masses of revolutionary workers, and in order to carry out resolutely the policy of 'taking firm hold of the revolution and promoting production' put forward by Chairman Mao, let us undertake widespread propaganda work and struggle, open fire fiercely and with still greater resolve at the bourgeois reactionary line, crush all new counter-attacks by the bourgeois reactionary line and launch a new upsurge in the Great Proletarian Cultural Revolution in the factories and plants!

In the boundless brilliance of the great thought of Mao Tse-tung, we look towards the future and see the magnificent prospect of the revolution. We the working class, poor and lower-middle peasants, and all working people must unite with the revolutionary students, intellectuals and cadres, must make a common effort, fight shoulder to shoulder and continue our victorious advances so as to carry the Great Proletarian Cultural Revolution through to the end!

Long live the Great Proletarian Cultural Revolution!

Long live the red sun in our hearts, the greatest leader Chairman Mao and long life, long, long life to him!

4 January   *The Shanghai Workers' Revolutionary Rebel*
1967   *General Headquarters and ten other revolu-*
                  tionary mass organizations

*

URGENT NOTICE

At present, when the Great Proletarian Cultural Revolution in Shanghai is entering the moment of decisive battle between the two lines, when the Shanghai Municipal Party Committee, which stubbornly clings to the bourgeois reactionary line, is being overthrown, the handful of Party persons in authority who are taking the capitalist road are once again hatching new plots. Colluding with the capitalist forces in society, they are making use of the problems concerning economic benefits to divert the general orientation of the struggle and to incite one group of people against another, causing breakdowns in factory production and railway and road traffic. They have even incited dockers to stop work, causing difficulties in running the port and damaging the international prestige of China. They are freely squandering the wealth of the state, arbitrarily increasing wages and material benefits, and granting all kinds of allowances and subsidies without limit, stirring people up to take over public buildings by force. These are the latest forms by which the Shanghai Municipal Party Committee persists in carrying out the bourgeois reactionary line.

In resorting to such base and treacherous means, the handful of Party persons in authority who are taking the capitalist road aim at none other than: (1) Setting themselves against Chairman Mao and the Party's Central Committee, and putting pressure on the Cultural Revolution Group under the Party's Central Committee by sabotaging production, interrupting communications and jeopardizing the national economy and the livelihood of the people, to attain their purpose of undermining the Great Proletarian Cultural Revolution; (2) Making use of economic benefits to divert the general orientation of the struggle in an attempt to shift the serious political struggle on to the wrong road of economic struggle, and at the same time to corrupt the revolutionary will of the masses by material gains, and to promote peaceful evolution and allow bourgeois ideas to run riot.

We hereby solemnly warn the Shanghai Municipal Party Committee that no plots will ever succeed that are aimed at diverting people's attention from the struggle through the disruption of production, interruption of communications and the increasing of wages and material benefits. The revolutionary rebels who are armed with Mao Tse-tung's Thought firmly expose this conspiracy and resolutely repulse the attacks by the bourgeois reactionary trend of thought. We must firmly implement the policy of 'taking firm hold of the revolution and promoting production' put forward by Chairman Mao and, on the one hand, take an active part in the Great Proletarian Cultural Revolution while on the other hand remain fast at our posts of production and construction, persist in the eight-hour work day, strive to fulfil and overfulfil production plans, and do our best to turn out high quality products. We believe that the masses of revolutionary workers have a high sense of political responsibility towards their great socialist motherland; they will certainly be able to put public interest to the fore, and, proceeding from the overall interests of the state, correctly handle the questions mentioned above and seize a double victory in the Cultural Revolution and in production.

In order swiftly to retrieve the grave situation in social production created by the Shanghai Municipal Party Committee, we appeal to comrades-in-arms of the revolutionary rebel groups of the whole city:

1. The workers, functionaries and students of revolutionary rebel groups must firmly carry through Chairman Mao's instruction of 'taking firm hold of the revolution and promoting production', take an active part in the great Cultural Revolution, and, at the same time, remain fast at their production posts and set an example in 'taking firm hold of the revolution and promoting production.'

2. They should appeal to all revolutionary rebels throughout the country to take prompt action to persuade those workers, functionaries, staff members of enterprises, and apprentices from Shanghai who are exchanging revolutionary experience in other parts of the country to return to Shanghai immediately, so that the great Cultural Revolution in their own units can proceed effectively and the 1967 production plans can be overfulfilled.

3. All certificates authorizing people to leave and exchange revolutionary experience in other parts of the country issued in the past by those in authority in the various organizations and enterprises are declared null and void on the day this document is published. These persons in authority should be made responsible for the return (by instalments if necessary) of the big sums of money issued to cover exchanges of experience (excluding transport fares).

4. Apart from necessary expenditure on production, wages, the Cultural Revolution, office administration and for other appropriate purposes, the circulating funds of all government offices, organizations and enterprises should be frozen as from the day of the publication of this document. This should be effected by the financial organizations at the municipal level and at all other levels under the joint supervision of the revolutionary

rebel groups and the revolutionary masses, so as to ensure that the economy of the state will not suffer losses (this does not apply to personal savings accounts).

5. To avoid shifting the general orientation of the struggle, matters related to the readjustment of wages, back payment of wages and material benefits, shall in principle be dealt with at a later stage of the movement. (Special cases shall be handled otherwise after asking the central authorities for instructions.)

6. The integration of students with workers and peasants is the inevitable road by which the students will transform their world outlook and successfully carry out the great Cultural Revolution. In order to stir up dissatisfaction among the workers against the students, to sabotage the integration of the students with the workers and to practise 'peaceful evolution' among the students, some persons in authority have gone to the length of paying the students relatively high wages for labour. This is entirely a revisionist practice, and should be stopped as from the day this notice is published.

7. All public buildings and houses confiscated from capitalists are the property of the whole people, and shall be handled in a unified way by the state at a later stage of the movement. No one is allowed to seize public buildings by force. After investigation, offenders shall be punished by the Public Security Bureau. Those who incite citizens to seize public buildings shall be dealt with by law in accordance with the gravity of the offence. Those who have moved into houses seized by force must move back to their original homes within one week.

8. Strengthen the dictatorship of the proletariat. Those who oppose Chairman Mao, Vice-Chairman Lin Piao, the Cultural Revolution Group under the Party's Central Committee, and those who undermine the great Cultural Revolution or sabotage production, shall be immediately arrested by the Public Security Bureau in accordance with the law. Those who in the course of the movement undermine social order, beat people up or commit atrocities, commit robbery or larceny must be dealt with by law in accordance with the gravity of the offence; stolen goods must be returned immediately. Those who repeat such offences or

after repeated education refuse to turn over a new leaf shall be severely punished.

9. The rebel organizations of various units and the revolutionary masses of the city are expected immediately to carry out the above points, and set in motion all organs of propaganda to publicize them and educate the masses.

10. The Municipal Party Committee and the Public Security Bureau are enjoined to act upon the above points. Those who act against the above points shall, after investigations, be immediately punished on charges of undermining the great Cultural Revolution.

9 January 1967   *The Shanghai Workers' Revolutionary Rebel General Headquarters and thirty-one other revolutionary mass organizations.*

*

MESSAGE OF GREETINGS TO REVOLUTIONARY REBEL ORGANIZATIONS IN SHANGHAI

To the Shanghai Workers' Revolutionary Rebel General Headquarters and thirty-one other revolutionary mass organizations:

Your 'Urgent Notice' issued on 9 January 1967, is indeed excellent. The guiding principles which you have put forward and the actions you have taken are entirely correct.

You have held aloft the great red banner of Mao Tse-tung's thought. You are models in creatively studying and applying Chairman Mao's works.

You have taken a firm stand on the side of the proletarian revolutionary line represented by Chairman Mao. You have seen through and exposed in time the schemes of the bourgeois reactionary line in starting a new counter-attack and have launched a forceful counter-offensive.

You have upheld the dictatorship of the proletariat, persisted in the general direction of socialism and put forward the fighting task of opposing the economism of counter-revolutionary revisionism.

You have formulated a correct policy in accordance with Chairman Mao's principle of 'taking firm hold of the revolution and promotion production'.

You have brought about a great alliance of the proletarian revolutionary organizations and become the nucleus uniting all revolutionary forces. You have taken firmly in your hands the destiny of the proletarian dictatorship, of the Great Proletarian Cultural Revolution and of the socialist economy.

All these revolutionary actions of yours have set a brilliant example for the working class and all labouring people and the revolutionary masses throughout the country.

We hereby call on Party, Government, Army and civilian circles, on the workers, peasants, revolutionary students, intellectuals and cadres throughout the country to learn from the experience of the revolutionary rebel groups in Shanghai, to take concerted action and to beat back the new counter-attack of the bourgeois reactionary line, so as to ensure that the Great Proletarian Cultural Revolution will forge ahead triumphantly along the proletarian revolutionary line represented by Chairman Mao.

11 January   *The Central Committee of the Chinese Com-*
1967   *munist Party.*
                  The State Council.
                  The Military Commission of the Central Com-
                  mittee of the Chinese Communist Party.
                  The Cultural Revolution Group under the
                  Central Committee of the Chinese Communist
                  Party.

TELEGRAM SALUTING CHAIRMAN MAO

Most, Most Respected and Beloved Chairman Mao:

We, fighters of the revolutionary rebel organizations in Shanghai, loyal to you for ever, extend our loftiest salute in the Great Proletarian Cultural Revolution to you, our great teacher, great leader, great supreme commander, and great helmsman, and the red sun that shines most brilliantly in our hearts.

Most, most respected and beloved Chairman Mao, we heard your voice from Peking – the Message of Greetings sent by the Central Committee of the Chinese Communist Party, the State Council, the Military Commission of the Central Committee of the Chinese Communist Party and the Cultural Revolution Group under the Party's Central Committee to the revolutionary rebel organizations in Shanghai, at the very moment when we were most enthusiastically acclaiming your decision to have broadcast to the whole country the 'Message to All Shanghai People' and the 'Urgent Notice', issued by the various revolutionary mass organizations here. This is a voice expressing the greatest concern and support for us, the voice of the greatest inspiration and encouragement to us. We rejoice and sing. Thousands of words would not suffice to express our happiness. Thousands of songs would not suffice to express our gratitude. We can only leap for joy and shout over and over again: Long live Chairman Mao! Long life and long, long life to him!

Most, most respected and beloved Chairman Mao, you always point out for us the general direction in which the struggle must go at the most critical moments of the revolution; you always give us boundless spiritual strength at the moment when the struggle grows sharpest. You always show warm solicitude and support for the revolutionary rebel groups. You always nurture and give active help to all new revolutionary things. At the present time, when we, the revolutionary rebel groups, are waging a fierce battle to deal severe blows at the new counter-attack of the bourgeois reactionary line, you have approved our general orientation, confirmed our fighting task and supported us in bringing about a great alliance of the proletarian revolutionary organizations and uniting all the revolutionary forces, so as to take firmly into our hands the destiny of the proletarian dictatorship, of the Great Proletarian Cultural Revolution and of the socialist economy. Your great and wise decision will quickly kindle the fierce flame spreading the all-encompassing class struggle throughout the country. All such things as counter-revolutionary economism, the new counter-attack organized by the representatives of the bourgeois reactionary line and the stubborn citadel of the bourgeois reactionary line will be utterly discredited and reduced to ashes in this raging fire.

You, most, most respected and beloved Chairman Mao, have repeatedly taught us that the enemy will not perish of himself nor will he step down from the stage of history of his own accord. The facts show this precisely. The counter-revolutionary scheme of economism concocted by the handful of persons in authority who are taking the capitalist road and the extremely small number of diehards who cling to the bourgeois reactionary line within the Shanghai Municipal Committee of the Chinese Communist Party has been exposed; they have been surrounded by the revolutionary masses ring upon ring and have begun to collapse along the whole front, but they are still struggling frantically and are trying by every means possible to break up the great alliance of our revolutionary groups in Shanghai in a vain attempt to create splits and stir up disputes among our revolutionary rebel organizations. In this way, they hope to slip through, get an opportunity to catch their breath and stage a come-back. We must not allow this scheme to succeed. We must follow your instructions: 'With power and to spare we must pursue the tottering foe and not ape Hsiang Yu the conqueror seeking idle fame',* take concerted action and vigorously pursue and fiercely beat 'the dogs in the water' and utterly defeat them, so that they can never rise again. We must firmly carry out the correct policy of 'Taking firm hold of the revolution and promoting production' advanced by you and thoroughly sweep away the bad influence of counter-revolutionary economism. We will not disappoint your expectations, and, under the great banner of Mao Tse-tung's Thought, we will unite more completely the revolutionary rebel groups, unite together the overwhelming majority of the masses and firmly hold the leadership of the Great Cultural

---

*From Chairman Mao's poem: *The Capture of Nanking by the People's Liberation Army*. '*The Conqueror*' was the self-bestowed title of Hsiang Yu, leader of a major peasant force against the Chin Dynasty in the third century B.C. Wishing to appear generous, he did not kill his rival Liu Pang when the opportunity offered. In the end, he was defeated by Liu Pang and committed suicide.

Revolution and production in Shanghai, so as to ensure that the Great Proletarian Cultural Revolution in the Shanghai area will forge ahead triumphantly along the proletarian revolutionary line represented by you!

Wishing our most, most respected and beloved great leader Chairman Mao a long, long life!

12 January 1967   *Rally held by the Revolutionary Rebel Organizations of Shanghai and the Shanghai Liaison Centres of Revolutionary Rebel Organizations of Other Places to Celebrate the Message of Greetings of the Central Authorities and Completely Smash the New Counter-Attack by the Bourgeois Revolutionary Line.*

*

OPPOSE ECONOMISM AND SMASH THE LATEST COUNTER-ATTACK BY THE BOURGEOIS REACTIONARY LINE

(Editorial of *Renmin Ribao* (*People's Daily*) and *Hongqi* (*Red Flag*), 12 January 1967)

The decision taken personally by our great leader, Chairman Mao to broadcast to the whole country the 'Message to All Shanghai People' and the 'Urgent Notice' issued by revolutionary mass organizations in Shanghai is an event of great historic importance. It marks the beginning of a new stage in our country's Great Proletarian Cultural Revolution.

The salient features of this new stage are:

The proletarian revolutionary line represented by Chairman Mao is being grasped to an ever greater extent by the broad masses. The citadels in which the bourgeois reactionary line has entrenched itself are being captured one by one.

The revolutionary movements of the workers, peasants and students and the revolutionary mass movement in the different fields of culture and in Party and government institutions are uniting into a mighty, irresistible revolutionary torrent. They are launching an all-out general offensive against the bourgeois reactionary line.

The forces of the revolutionary rebel groups of the proletariat are growing in scale and strength. They are arming themselves more fully with Mao Tse-tung's Thought in the course of the struggle, adhering firmly to the general orientation of the struggle, constantly improving the art of struggle and becoming the backbone force of the Great Proletarian Cultural Revolution.

The majority of the masses are becoming united, with the proletarian revolutionary rebel groups as their core. Under the leadership of the Party Central Committee headed by Chairman Mao, the revolutionary masses are taking into their own hands the destiny of the Great Proletarian Cultural Revolution, the destiny of the struggle [to overthrow those persons in authority who are taking the capitalist road], the criticism and repudiation [of the reactionary bourgeois academic 'authorities' and the ideology of the bourgeoisie and all other exploiting classes] and the transformation [of education, literature and art and all other parts of the superstructure not in correspondence with the socialist economic base], the destiny of production and work, and the destiny of the proletarian dictatorship and the socialist state.

Under the impact of this mighty, irresistible revolutionary torrent, the handful of Party persons in authority who are taking the capitalist road and an extremely small number of diehards stubbornly pursuing the bourgeois reactionary line are being forced to retreat from one position to another. Their ferocious, counter-revolutionary features have been or are being exposed. Heavily besieged by the revolutionary masses, they have begun to collapse all along the line.

However, will these reactionary elements lay down their arms and surrender of their own accord? Will they step down from the stage of history of their own accord? No! They will never do so! Like all other reactionaries in the past, they will never lay down their arms and surrender or step down from the stage of history of their own accord.

As Chairman Mao has taught us:

The enemy will not perish of himself. Neither the Chinese reactionaries nor the aggressive forces of U.S. imperialism in China will step down from the stage of history of their own accord. *

Everything reactionary is the same; if you don't hit it, it won't fall. This is also like sweeping the floor; as a rule, where the broom does not reach, the dust will not vanish of itself.†

The reality of the development of China's Great Proletarian Cultural Revolution is a further proof of this brilliant thesis of Chairman Mao's.

In capturing each fortress, the revolutionary fighters will meet frenzied resistance from the class enemy. At every step forward taken by the revolution, the enemy will play new tricks and resort to whatever schemes they can devise. When one way fails, they fall back on another. When tough tactics do not work, they try kid-glove ones. When force fails, they use non-violent methods. They also mix tough with kid-glove tactics and combine force with non-violence. Their speciality is to wave 'red flags' to oppose the red flag and to instigate one section of the masses to fight against another. More often than not, they cunningly take over the revolutionary slogans raised by the Party Central Committee and Chairman Mao and distort them to serve their counterrevolutionary political purposes. They are now appearing to be ultra 'Left' and pretending to hoist the flag of 'opposition to the bourgeois reactionary line' in order to hoodwink and deceive part of the masses. They call white black and divert the struggle in the wrong direction by turning its spearhead against the proletarian revolutionary line, the proletarian revolutionary headquarters and the revolutionary masses, by which means they seek to protect themselves and the bourgeois reactionary line and to preserve the old capitalist and revisionist order.

At the present time, the handful of Party persons in authority

* Mao Tse-tung, 'Carry the Revolution Through to the End', *Selected Works*, English edn., Foreign Languages Press, Peking, 1961, Vol. IV, p. 301.

† Mao Tse-tung, 'The Situation and Our Policy After the Victory in the War of Resistance Against Japan', *Selected Works*, English edn., Foreign Languages Press, Peking, 1961, Vol. IV, p. 19.

who are taking the capitalist road and the extremely small number of diehards stubbornly pursuing the bourgeois reactionary line are colluding with bourgeois elements, speculators, landlords, rich peasants, counter-revolutionaries, bad elements and Rightists in society and using economism to deceive the masses and incite them to undermine production, disrupt financial work and sabotage the Great Proletarian Cultural Revolution and to wage a struggle against the great, glorious and correct Chinese Communist Party and against our socialist state of the proletarian dictatorship.

The 'Urgent Notice' issued by the Shanghai Workers' Revolutionary Rebel General Headquarters and the other revolutionary mass organizations in Shanghai has vividly and penetratingly revealed the big conspiracy of the reactionary elements in the Shanghai area – the conspiracy of using the 'sugar-coated bullets' of economic benefits to lure a part of the masses. The reactionary elements freely squander the wealth of the state, arbitrarily increase wages and benefits, wantonly distribute all kinds of funds and materials and stir up the masses to take over public buildings by force and occupy them as their own private property. They instigate acts of violence, create incidents, incite a number of workers to desert their posts in production, thus bringing some factories to a standstill and disrupting railway and road traffic. They even incite harbour personnel to stop work. Some leading members of the railway departments use similar means to disrupt rail transport in a vain attempt to sabotage the Great Proletarian Cultural Revolution. The reactionary elements think they are clever, but in fact they are lifting a rock only to drop it on their own feet. The more actively they operate, the more revealed are their counter-revolutionary revisionist features. In this way they are creating the conditions for their own total collapse.

The game of economism that these people are playing has provided the revolutionary masses with very good teaching material by negative example. It has enabled them to recognize the real nature of economism and the need to expose and attack it until it is utterly crushed.

What kind of stuff is economism?

It is a form of bribery that caters to the psychology of a few backward people among the masses, corrupts the masses' revolutionary will and leads their political struggle on to the wrong road of economism, luring them to seek only personal and short-term interests in disregard of the interests of the state and the collective and the long-term interests. Its aim is to strangle the Great Proletarian Cultural Revolution, to disintegrate the dictatorship of the proletariat and the socialist system.

Economism disrupts social production, the national economy and socialist ownership. It promotes the tendency towards the spontaneous development of capitalism and encourages revisionist material incentives in a vain attempt to destroy the economic basis of socialism.

Economism is opposed to Marxism-Leninism, Mao Tse-tung's thought; it is out-and-out counter-revolutionary revisionist stuff. It is garbage picked up from the rubbish dump of old-time and modern revisionism. Under the capitalist system, economism is an instrument for preserving the reactionary rule of capitalism and opposing the proletarian revolution. Under the socialist system, it has an even more reactionary nature and is an instrument for counter-revolutionary capitalist restoration.

In a word, economism substitutes bourgeois spontaneity for proletarian revolutionary consciousness, substitutes bourgeois ultra-democracy for proletarian democratic centralism and proletarian sense of organization and discipline, substitutes bourgeois reactionary illegalities for proletarian dictatorship and its extensive democracy, and substitutes capitalist ownership for socialist ownership. Economism is a new form in which the bourgeois reactionary line launches a big counter-attack against the proletarian revolutionary line.

All revolutionary people and all revolutionary organizations must heighten their vigilance a hundredfold, see through the class enemy's schemes of economism, completely smash the latest counter-attack by the bourgeois reactionary line and carry the Great Proletarian Cultural Revolution through to the end.

The 'Urgent Notice' issued by the revolutionary mass organizations in Shanghai holds high the great red banner of the proletarian revolutionary line represented by Chairman Mao and resolutely upholds the correct policy of 'taking firm hold of the revolution and promoting production' advanced by Chairman Mao, thus setting a good example for the struggle against counter-revolutionary economism, or, in other words, against counter-revolutionary revisionism.

In their 'Message of Greetings to Revolutionary Rebel Organizations in Shanghai', the Central Committee of the Chinese Communist Party, the State Council, the Military commission of the Central Committee of the Chinese Communist Party and the Cultural Revolution Group under the Party's Central Committee call on Party, Government, Army and civilian circles, on the workers, peasants, and revolutionary students, intellectuals and cadres throughout the country to learn from the experience of the Shanghai revolutionary rebels, to take concerted action and beat back the latest counter-attack by the bourgeois reactionary line, so that the Great Proletarian Cultural Revolution will forge ahead triumphantly along the proletarian revolutionary line represented by Chairman Mao. This call will undoubtedly be a great encouragement to the working class and the revolutionary people throughout the country.

In order to smash economism completely, all proletarian revolutionaries should, in the manner of the revolutionary rebels in Shanghai, bring their forces into closer alliance under the great banner of Mao Tse-tung's Thought and take the leadership of the Great Cultural Revolution and of production firmly into their own hands.

We must carry on patient and painstaking political-ideological work among those people who are temporarily hoodwinked. We must have the conviction that the overwhelming majority of them want to make revolution. The moment they comprehend the truth, they will be able to distinguish clearly between right and wrong on cardinal issues and take their stand on the side of the proletarian revolutionary line represented by Chairman Mao.

The present all-embracing class struggle has been provoked

by the bourgeoisie and their agents. To those who obstinately cling to the bourgeois reactionary line, we give the following warning: pull back right away from the brink of the abyss while there is still a chance to atone for your crimes before the Party and the people by rendering valuable service. If you do not surrender to the revolutionary people, then you will be ruined.

Let the working class unite!

Let the working class, the poor peasants and the lower-middle class peasants and all other working people unite!

Let all working people unite with the revolutionary students, revolutionary intellectuals and revolutionary cadres!

People of all nationalities, unite!

Unfold the all-embracing class struggle on a nationwide scale!

Totally smash the latest counter-attack by the bourgeois reactionary line!

Carry the Great Proletarian Cultural Revolution through to the end!

Long live Chairman Mao, the great teacher, great leader, great supreme commander and great helmsman!

*

PROLETARIAN REVOLUTIONARIES, UNITE

(By Commentator, *Hongqi*, No. 2, 1967)

The golden monkey wrathfully swung his massive cudgel,
And the jade-like firmament was cleared of dust.*

Guided by the proletarian revolutionary line represented by Chairman Mao Tse-tung, the glorious Shanghai working class has formed a million-strong, mighty army of revolutionary rebels. In alliance with other revolutionary organizations, they have been meeting head-on the new counter-attacks by the bourgeois reactionary line, seizing power from the handful of Party persons in authority who are taking the capitalist road, and establishing the new order of the Great Proletarian Cultural

*From Chairman Mao's poem: *Reply to Comrade Kuo Mo-jo.*

Revolution. With an irresistible, sweeping force, they are following up this victory and brushing aside the rubbish that stands in the way of the wheel of history.

This revolutionary action of the working class and other revolutionary masses and revolutionary cadres in Shanghai marks a new turning point in our country's Great Proletarian Cultural Revolution and the beginning of a new stage in this revolution. This is a great new victory for Mao Tse-tung's thought.

The revolutionary principle adopted, and the revolutionary actions taken, by the working class and other revolutionary masses and the revolutionary cadres in Shanghai have set an example for the whole country and provided invaluable new experience for the Great Proletarian Cultural Revolution.

Their experience is many-sided. It boils down to one point: that proletarian revolutionaries, forming an alliance, have seized power from the handful of Party persons who were in authority and took the capitalist road, and held the political, economic and cultural power of the Shanghai municipality firmly in their own hands.

Marxism-Leninism, Mao Tse-tung's thought, teaches us that the basic question of a revolution is that of political power. The central task of the Great Proletarian Cultural Revolution, in the last analysis, is the struggle by which the proletariat seizes power from the handful of Party persons in authority who are taking the capitalist road. This is the focal point of the class struggle in our country at the present stage, a concentrated expression of the struggle between the socialist and capitalist roads.

On 1 June 1966, our great leader Chairman Mao personally decided to have the text broadcast of a big-character poster from Peking University, the first Marxist-Leninist poster in the country. This was in support of the struggle of the proletarian revolutionaries of Peking University to seize power from the Lu Ping anti-party clique in the university. It was a great strategic move which kindled the flames of the Great Proletarian Cultural Revolution now raging throughout the country.

Now our great leader Chairman Mao himself has decided to give publicity over the radio to the 'Message to All Shanghai

People' and the 'Urgent Notice' issued by Shanghai's revolutionary mass organizations. This is in support of the struggle of the working class and other revolutionary masses and revolutionary cadres in Shanghai who united to seize power in the municipality from the handful of Party persons who were in authority and took the capitalist road and the extremely small number of diehards who persistently pursued the bourgeois reactionary line. It is yet another great strategic measure taken in the new situation, one which will stimulate a new leap in the Great Proletarian Cultural Revolution throughout the country.

Those Party persons in authority who are taking the capitalist road are just a handful, but in varying degrees they still hold Party, political and financial power in the localities and units where they are entrenched. They always use this power to attack the masses and undermine the Great Proletarian Cultural Revolution.

How do they use their power to undermine the Great Proletarian Cultural Revolution?

They use the Party power in their hands to deceive, hoodwink and repress a number of cadres and Party and Youth League members. They attempt to break down our Party's extremely strict proletarian discipline which is based on Mao Tse-tung's thought, that discipline which is essential for the proletariat to defeat the bourgeoisie. They distort our Party's discipline into bourgeois discipline, into 'discipline' to oppose the Party, socialism and Mao Tse-tung's thought, into 'discipline' to resist the proletarian revolutionary line represented by Chairman Mao, turning it into a 'charm' for repressing the masses and opposing the revolution. They condemn whoever opposes them as an 'anti-Party' element.

Making use of the political power they exercise in those departments and localities under their control, this handful of persons practise bourgeois dictatorship to suppress the revolutionary masses wherever they can. They brand as a 'counter-revolutionary' anyone who rises up and rebels against them, and even dismiss or imprison him. They incite the masses to struggle against each other. They use the slogan 'Defend the proletarian dictatorship!' in a distorted way to deceive certain people into establishing under their control such organizations as 'the army of defenders of red state power' to protect themselves.

This handful of persons use the financial power in their hands to get certain befuddled people to protect them. They use money to buy over people so as to corrupt the revolutionary masses. They make use of economic measures of all kinds in an attempt to lead some people on to the evil road of economism, of pursuing purely immediate individual interests. They want not only to restore but even to extend some erroneous measures adopted in the past in regard to wage and welfare systems. They issue cheques and materials freely, in an effort to win the hearts of the people by liberally giving away what belongs to the state. In doing so, they attempt to sabotage production, finances and communications and transport. With malicious intentions they 'pass on the contradictions to their superiors'. These are the current manifestations of the death-bed struggle of the handful of Party persons in authority who are taking the capitalist road. It represents a counter-attack in a new form by the bourgeois reactionary line at the present time.

These people protect every old vestige of capitalism and revisionism; in the final analysis, they are protecting their own power. In the face of pressure from the revolutionary masses, they may make this or that false 'concession'. But whatever they do is aimed at attacking our dictatorship of the proletariat and preserving their power to suppress the masses. On the question of power, they struggle for every bit of it and never make any concession. They attempt to take all possible measures to disrupt our socialist national economic life so as to achieve their goal of preserving their own power.

The most fundamental thing in our struggle against this handful of persons is to wrest power from them. Only when their power is seized and dictatorship is exercised over them will they be completely refuted, overthrown and utterly discredited.

Chairman Mao teaches us that to wrest power from these persons means the revolution of one class to overthrow another class under the conditions of the dictatorship of the proletariat, i.e., a revolution of the proletariat to liquidate the bourgeoisie.

The struggle between the proletarian revolutionaries and the handful of Party persons in authority who are taking the capitalist road is acute, complicated and tortuous. The strongholds in which the counter-revolutionary revisionists are entrenched must be seized, one by one. The positions recovered by the proletariat must also be consolidated, one by one.

We must heighten our vigilance against cunning enemies. Hypocritically, they have raised the flag of 'revolution' to wrest power from the proletariat. They are accustomed to fabricating rumours, sowing discord, transposing black and white, confusing right and wrong, and instigating the masses so as to divert the struggle in the wrong direction and turn the spearhead of attack against revolutionaries, the dictatorship of the proletariat and the revolutionary headquarters of the proletariat. All revolutionary comrades must follow Chairman Mao's teachings, keep their eyes open, and distinguish between the enemy and ourselves, and between right and wrong on vital questions. Those bad elements who behind our backs stir up the winds of evil and turn the spearhead against the dictatorship of the proletariat and the proletarian revolutionary headquarters must be firmly exposed and overthrown, one by one.

The great contribution of the Shanghai working class and other revolutionary masses and revolutionary cadres is that they have taken a firm stand on the side of the proletarian revolutionary line represented by Chairman Mao, fearlessly launched an extensive counter-attack against the new counter-offensive of the bourgeois reactionary line, provided experience in seizing power – under the conditions of the dictatorship of the proletariat – from the handful of Party persons in authority who are taking the capitalist road, and advanced correct principles and policies, correct forms of organization and correct methods of struggle.

These are the most essential things worth studying by Party, Government, Army and civilian circles, by workers, peasants, and revolutionary students, intellectuals, and cadres throughout the country.

The great revolution in Shanghai is an embodiment of the leading role and the initiative of the working class, their sense of revolutionary organization and discipline, and it has developed extensive democracy under the dictatorship of the proletariat.

Shanghai's experience proves that only by seizing power from the handful of Party persons in authority who are taking the capitalist road, and strengthening the dictatorship of the proletariat can extensive proletarian democracy be ensured.

Shanghai's experience proves that extensive democracy under the dictatorship of the proletariat is by no means ultra-democracy or 'small group' mentality [considering only the interests of a small group and ignoring the overall interest – Ed.]. Only by giving effect to democratic centralism and the great alliance of proletarian revolutionaries under the banner of Mao Tse-tung's thought can there be extensive democracy under the dictatorship of the proletariat, can excellent battles be fought with concentrated forces and can new revolutionary order be established.

Shanghai's experience proves that the principle of 'taking firm hold of the revolution and promoting production' advanced by the Party's Central Committee represented by Chairman Mao must be firmly grasped, that resolute and uncompromising struggles must be waged against all sorts of bourgeois revisionist economism, anarchism, liberalization, etc., and that the general orientation of socialism must be maintained and socialist ownership must be upheld; only this can be called extensive democracy under the dictatorship of the proletariat.

The aim of Shanghai's revolutionary masses in practising extensive democracy under the dictatorship of the proletariat is very clear. It is to arouse the masses to topple the handful of Party persons in authority who are taking the capitalist road, and the ghosts and monsters in society, and uphold and develop the politics, economy and culture of socialism.

The message of greetings to the revolutionary rebel organizations in Shanghai from the Central Committee of the Chinese Communist Party, the State Council, the Military Commission of the Party Central Committee and the Cultural Revolution Group under the Party Central Committee states:

You have brought about a great alliance of the proletarian revolutionary organizations and become the nucleus uniting all revolutionary forces. You have taken firmly in your hands the destiny of the proletarian dictatorship, of the Great Proletarian Cultural Revolution and of the socialist economy.

This is a high appraisal of the Shanghai proletarian revolutionaries, as well as a great call to the revolutionary people throughout the country.

The latest counter-attacks by the bourgeois reactionary line do not indicate that this handful of reactionaries are powerful but that they are having fits of hysteria. Such fits merely point to their imminent collapse.

Our dictatorship of the proletariat is strong and firm. We have the powerful People's Liberation Army which is infinitely loyal to Chairman Mao and to the people. We have hundreds of millions of people armed with Mao Tse-tung's Thought. This is the greatest force capable of vanquishing all enemies.

We must bear in mind this teaching of Chairman Mao's:

'All views that overestimate the strength of the enemy and underestimate the strength of the people are wrong'.*

We are facing an excellent situation, a situation full of brightness. We must grasp 'the essential fact that the enemy is nearing extinction while they the revolutionaries themselves are approaching victory'.† Like the revolutionary masses in Shanghai, we must courageously beat back the challenges of the handful of agents of the bourgeoisie. We must dare to struggle and be good at struggle, dare to win victory and be good at winning victory.

Proletarian revolutionaries, unite and rally with the broad masses, and, led by the great supreme commander Chairman Mao carry on an all-round class struggle throughout the country!

Resolutely carry out the principle of 'taking firm hold of the

*Mao Tse-tung, 'The Present Situation and Our Tasks', *Selected Works*, English edn., Foreign Languages Press, Peking, 1961, Vol. IV, p. 173.

†Mao Tse-tung, 'The Turning Point in World War II', *Selected Works*, English edn., Foreign Languages Press, Peking, 1965, Vol. III, p. 103.

revolution and promoting production' advanced by Chairman
Mao!

Crush the latest counter-attacks of the bourgeois reactionary
line!

Crush bourgeois economism!

Resolutely seize power from the handful of Party persons in
authority who are taking the capitalist road!

Long live the dictatorship of the proletariat!

Long live the ever-victorious thought of Mao Tse-tung!

5. The Great Strategic Plan

This directive was issued on 7 March 1967. The re-opening
of schools at that time was only partially effective. The work
of the PLA in the educational field was renewed in the
autumn.

A DIRECTIVE FROM CHAIRMAN MAO CONCERNING THE GREAT STRATEGIC PLAN FOR THE GREAT PROLETARIAN CULTURAL REVOLUTION*

Comrades Lin Piao, En-lai and the Comrades of the Cultural
Revolution Group:

This document could be distributed to the whole country to
be acted upon accordingly. The Army should give military and
political training in the universities, middle schools and the
higher classes of primary schools, stage by stage and group by
group. It should help in re-opening school classes, strengthening
organization, setting up the leading bodies on the principle of the
'three-in-one' combination and carrying out the task of 'struggle-
criticism-transformation'. It should first make experiments at
selected points and acquire experience and then popularize it step
by step. And the students should be persuaded to implement the
teaching of Marx that only by emancipating all mankind can the
proletariat achieve its own final emancipation, and in military

*The translation was published in *Peking Review*, 15 March 1968.

and political training, they should not exclude those teachers and cadres who have made mistakes. Apart from the aged and the sick, these people should be allowed to take part so as to facilitate their remoulding. Provided all this is done conscientiously, it is not difficult to solve the problems

7 March   MAO TSE-TUNG

4

REPORTS AND CONVERSATIONS

THE atmosphere at a visit to a factory or an institute has changed since the Cultural Revolution began. Formerly the foreign visitors were shown into a special room, often furnished with upholstered chairs with lace antimacassars. Cups of tea were served and cigarettes offered. Several representatives of the enterprise were present, but only one speaker, the director or secretary of the Party Committee, gave the prepared report and answered questions. The rest sat silent, taking time, presumably, from other duties.

This ceremony and waste of space and time was one of the objects of criticism at the Second Machine Tool Factory at Peking. Now the visitors sit on benches and the room is evidently used for working meetings. The visit opens with reading some quotations from the little red book. (The interpreter finds the place in the English edition for the visitors.) Workers from the new rebel committee are the hosts. The conversation is informal. One speaker leads but others chip in. The atmosphere is frank and open. At a college, the students have no hesitation in giving their views in front of professors, who were formerly treated with deference and awe. On the other hand, a large part of the conversation is in set phrases and generalizations. This is not, I think, a cover for individual opinions. It is rather that, for the speakers, to be able to analyse their own experience in terms of 'the choice between two roads', 'eradicating revisionism', or 'avoiding the ultra-left line' is for themselves a source of enlightenment and they think it more important to give the generalizations than the concrete experience. It only needs a little probing to bring out the concrete experience. A comical example from a commune:

'Formerly we fed the pigs on grain; that is the rich way. Now we contribute to national development by feeding them economically.'

'How do you feed them?'

'We feed them diligently and economically.'

'Yes, but what do you give them to eat?'

'We give them one quarter of the grain, and we cut green food in the ditches.'

'How do the pigs like it?'

'They put on weight faster than before.'

The following are a few typical examples of reports on revolutionary experience given to me in October and November 1967, supplemented from notes taken by Mr Roland Berger on an earlier and a later tour.

A Machine Tool Factory, Peking

The movement in this factory took light from the publication on 2 June of the poster at Peking University. Thousands of posters were put up criticizing the authorities. One in particular, who was considered a bad egg, was the Deputy Chief Engineer, who had a suspicious past – he had been an officer under the Kuomintang and he was a capitalist, receiving interest. (Under the state-private system which was introduced in 1956, many capitalists received interest on the value of assets in the factories which they formerly owned, and many were employed in executive jobs. There does not seem to have been any decree winding up this system, but it seems to have generally melted in the fire of the Cultural Revolution.) The authorities were criticized for their personal attitude. They made themselves superior and lived in a bourgeois style. There was an accident when a worker was drowned in trying to save a boy who fell into the river, while one of the cadres who was having a swim near by gave no help and behaved in a heartless manner. One of them used his office car to go fishing on Sunday. He arranged for his wife to have an administrative job for which she was in no way qualified. When they were expected to do the regular stint of manual labour in the factory they chose clean and light work for themselves and arranged to be in the workshop that has to be kept at a steady temperature for technical reasons. They were accused of an undemocratic style of management, which was inherited from the Soviets, relying on experts and giving orders without explanation to the workers. They were accused of misusing the factory funds – spending money on repairing the swimming pool and prettyfying the office, not caring for production.

(The mildness of the degree of corruption which raised so much indignation is typical of the high level of probity generally established in China.)

The outburst of criticism led to a work team being sent in by the Peking Municipal Party Committee, on 8 June. (This is an old established method in the Chinese Communist Party. When there is trouble at one level, a work team is sent in from a higher level to investigate and settle the problem.) The work team met the workers at the factory; they declared that they had come to help to carry on the Cultural Revolution. 'Your Party Committee in the factory,' they said, 'is basically revolutionary and good; the Cultural Revolution is primarily concerned with cultural matters. It is an affair of the universities not of industry.' The rebels were indignant. The work team was defending the Party Committee. They were refusing to respond to Chairman Mao's call. That night hundreds of posters went up criticizing the work team.

Since the rebels were not silenced, a second work team was sent in. They had been briefed by the first, and learning by that experience, they changed their tactics. They pretended to support the revolutionary movement. They set up a committee of twenty-three members. It was in name a Revolutionary Committee but the members were carefully chosen by the work team. Its members were Party cadres and staff of the factory, leaving no room for workers. It soon became clear that this work team, like the first, was trying to smother the revolutionary movement.

On 23 June the workers organized a committee of their own of eighteen members. They called a meeting to dissolve the committee of twenty-three and to expel the work team. At 10 o'clock that night a third work team was sent in. This team, without pretence, attacked the rebel workers. They branded the group of eighteen as counter-revolutionaries and described the incident of 23 June as a small Hungarian rising. To oppose the work team, they said, is opposing the Central Committee, and opposing the Central Committee is opposing Chairman Mao. Many workers were astonished at this attack. The work team, however, succeeded in organizing groups of workers who were blindly loyal to the Party (the rebels describe them as conservatives or royalists) to criticize the group of eighteen and to oppose those who put up posters critical of the authorities.

The work team on 24 June held a great meeting. They called on the eighteen to recant. They tried to make them confess that they were mere self-seekers aiming to set themselves up as leaders. They visited their families and urged them to have nothing to do with such counter-revolutionaries. The work team, throughout the argument, took on themselves the mantle of the Party. They exploited the loyalty of the workers to the Party and their devotion to Chairman Mao. Many were taken in by them.

This was the period described as the white terror. The rebels were under heavy pressure – the hardest thing to bear was the attempt to get at their families. A small resolute group stuck to their opinions.

At the beginning of August the scene changed. Chairman Mao returned to Peking. After a stormy meeting of the Central Committee lasting ten days, the Sixteen Points were issued. While the session was going on Chairman Mao put up his own poster – 'Bombard the Headquarters'. Now it became clear to the workers that the work team had turned things upside down. The work team were unrepentant when they finally left the factory on 13 August; they maintained that, though they might have had some shortcomings in matters of detail, there was no mistake in their line. They advised the authorities in the factory to concentrate all their forces to discredit and crush the rebel group.

The rebels, however, were heartened by the lead that Chairman Mao was giving to the Cultural Revolution; a new group was set up with at first five members. They re-examined the incident of 23 June and restored the good name of those who had been branded as counter-revolutionary. The group quickly grew ('A single spark may start a prairie fire') but all through the summer contention went on. While they argued, the workers kept up production. The rebels put in extra work to make up for time lost at meetings. They were under high pressure. Sometimes they got only two hours of sleep. The authorities resorted to 'economism' and tried to get the apprentices on their side by offering them full wages, but they did not have much success.

By November a majority of the workers had been won over by the rebels; on 25 November the workers, by direct election 'in the manner of the Paris Commune' set up a Revolutionary Committee but the management of the factory was still in the hands of the authorities. It was not until January 1967, following the 'January Storm' in Shanghai, that the workers seized power and set up their own management.

In October 1967, when I visited the factory, authority was in the hands of the Triple Combination. The first element in this is revolutionary cadres. Some had early been condemned by the work teams – that is to say, they sympathized with the rebels. Some had followed the authorities but had since admitted their mistakes. Only two of the old bosses had been finally condemned, and were then working on the shop floor, being given an opportunity to 'remould their thoughts by productive labour'.

The second element in the Triple Combination is representatives of the workers – these were men who had come to the fore during the struggle. The third is representatives of the militia. The emphasis at that time was on unity and reconciliation.

The Revolutionary Committee was in charge of management. The work was carried out by three offices, Politics, Administration, and Production. The head of each office serves on the Committee.

The State plan is given to the office of production; the workers, technicians and cadres consult with each other to improve efficiency. The factory is proud to claim that during the period of struggle in July 1967 they produced a new type of grinder, of an international standard.

Production generally has increased. Instead of the artificial system of the staff being required to put in a month of work during the year, the technicians and cadres now regularly work a full shift once or twice a week, so that they have a real knowledge both of the workers and of the technical problems that crop up. Decisions can be taken quickly and a lot of red tape has been cut out.

The workers hope to continue to increase production as well as to carry forward the reorganization of political life. 'To seize power is difficult. To use it well is still more difficult.'

A Sweet Factory, Shanghai

At the other extreme of the industrial spectrum is a small sweet factory in Shanghai employing 250 workers. It belonged to a capitalist and was taken into the state-private system in 1956. In September 1966 it was taken over completely. The capitalist who, under the state-private system got his 5 per cent amounting to 360 yuan per month, has been expropriated, but he is still allowed 160 yuan per month, which is considered adequate for him to support a family of six, taking into account the fact that one son is earning.

When the factory was taken over in 1956 all production was by hand. Technical innovations were made in 1958; now it is about 40 per cent mechanized. About 30 per cent of the output is exported to South-East Asia.

The course of the Cultural Revolution in this small enterprise followed the general line in the city. The workers began to criticize the cadres. The Party branch took a reactionary stand. In November 1966 the rebels in the factory appealed to the Headquarters in the city for support. In January 1967, in the 'great storm' they seized power.

At first the workers tried to run everything themselves, but they found that it was necessary to make use of the experience and ability of the cadres. The question now came up, how to treat cadres who had been on the reactionary side during the struggle. The workers studied the directive in the Sixteen Points, articles in the press on the question of cadres and the quotations from Chairman Mao's writings. They understood that it is necessary to allow the cadres to correct their mistakes. They analysed the history and attitudes of their own cadres.

The Vice Director (who was sitting at the table while this conversation went on) had been on the wrong side; he had fermented disputes among the workers; but when the rebels took power he came over to them. They looked into his past life. He came from a poor peasant family and he had been a child beggar. At the age of 13 he became a landlord's servant (a kind of domestic slave). At 16 he joined the PLA. He became a Party member at 18. His work in the factory had been under the guidance of the Party and he could not be too much blamed for loyalty to his superiors. He was classed, in the categories of the Sixteen Points, as comparatively good.

The Secretary of the Party branch had taken a strong line against the rebels. She sowed dissension among the workers and branded the leaders of the rebels as 'ghosts and monsters'. (This phrase of Mao's, an allusion to folk lore, is intended to apply to evil remnants of the old feudal and bourgeois society.) When she was accused of having made mistakes, she resisted stubbornly, and abused the rebels and Party members who were supporting them.

They analysed her life story. She had been a child worker and had suffered bitter oppression. When she joined the Party she set herself up as a superior person, she divorced herself from the workers and carried out her responsibilities in an undemocratic style. They decided that she was not basically anti-socialist; she was placed in the third category, as one who had made serious mistakes. In the end she recognized her mistakes and made a self criticism. She was brought in to the Triple Combination, and is now in charge of propaganda.

The former Director of the factory made serious mistakes. He was slack in his Party work and let in untrustworthy ex-bourgeois characters. He believed in co-existence with the old capitalist and allowed him to run the supply department of the factory. He was accused also of putting 'feudal' designs, of dragons and fairies, on the wrapping paper of the sweets.

In management, he followed 'revisionist' policies. He did not take the workers into his confidence. He told them to trust the capitalist and built up his authority. He told the workers that without the capitalist they could not produce sweets, though in fact they had improved the quality of their products since the factory had been taken over. He did not put politics first, but, following the Liu-Teng line, subordinated the workers to the technicians, and set up profits as the criterion of success; also he made use of a system of incentive wages. He came from a bourgeois family and lived in a bourgeois style. He had close relations with capitalists – dined with them and exchanged gifts.

He was graded as a man who had made serious mistakes and as a bourgeois who had not sufficiently remoulded himself, but he was not branded as an anti-Party Rightist. They propose to help him recognize his mistakes. He is difficult to help because he is afraid of losing face, but they consider that he has made some progress. He and the old capitalist are now working on the shop floor.

The system of management has been simplified and the number of cadres reduced by 42 per cent. Each team of workers has a leader who looks after production. Unnecessary rules have been abolished. Both quality and quantity of output have been markedly improved; the annual plan of output was being over-fulfilled. Even in the hectic month of January 1967, output was above the planned level.

The wage system has not yet been altered. The average wage is 70 yuan per month. A worker who has been with the factory for fifteen years has a right to a pension on retirement of 75 per cent of earnings. Veteran workers receive full pay during sickness; others, 50 per cent of earnings.

The former Trade Union worked on the Liu-Teng line and has been repudiated by the workers.

The factory is now managed by a committee of eleven members. Some 60 per cent of the workers are women but there are only three women on the committee.

This story provides a picture of the high degree of devolution and workers' self-management that is being established in the process of the Cultural Revolution. The workers accept guidance from the cadres because they find that they need it.

This kind of self-management is very different from the Yugoslav system which gives representatives of the workers control over prices and the commodities to be produced, and it is different also from the experimental systems in the Soviet Union and the People's Democracies which instruct the management of enterprises to earn profits. Prices and supplies are given to an enterprise in China; in the case of this sweet factory, the plan is given by the Shanghai Food Corporation; the product mix is controlled by market demand; if actual costs are kept below the planned level, the extra profit is not kept by the enterprise, but costs and prices are reckoned to include the social security payments for which the enterprise is responsible. Management is not concerned with commercial affairs, but purely with production and human relations within the factory. 'Putting politics in command' means that pride rather than money earnings gives the incentive to the workers and management alike to maintain and improve production.

A Transport Company, Peking

The following conversation is reported by Roland Berger. The trucking company is mainly concerned with carrying agricultural produce from communes around Peking. The staff consists of drivers, porters, service and repair workers. A group reported on a ten-day course on the Thought of Mao Tse-tung which they had just completed. They were about eight truck drivers and two mechanics. Other groups were to follow on similar study courses.

Each of them spoke of the value of the course of study to their thinking and attitudes.

A driver, aged 26, from a poor peasant family:

... I thought that I had come from a poor peasant family, so naturally I should be a genuine, spontaneous red. I took part in the Cultural Revolution with the idea of being a spontaneous red. I thought I did not need to remould my ideas or make revolution against myself. Owing to these ideas I was influenced by the bourgeois reactionary line.

The masses were incited to struggle against each other and I branded my own class brothers as reactionary. I even beat them up. After I had made such mistakes, many of my workmates in the company tried to help me. Although I made self-criticism, I was not really persuaded in my heart. The main thing was that my world outlook was not sufficiently remoulded.

At the very beginning of the study of Mao I was not willing to participate because I took the wrong attitude towards the study class. I was afraid of being criticized and repudiated by others.

But through this study I have come to understand that the attitude I took at the beginning was wrong. The main purpose of the class is not to criticize and repudiate people. These classes are completely in accord with the Sixteen Points to let the masses liberate themselves. I understood better what is meant by 'the people' and 'the enemy'. I was confused on the question of class origin – that it is important but that the key question is what a comrade does. Chairman Mao's statement clarified this for me. After studying these passages I was inspired and began to understand that those who come from a bad family class origin but who at the beginning of the Cultural Revolution stood on the proletarian line, were in the first rank of the struggle.

I also studied Norman Bethune. He had come to China and sacrificed his life – here am I a Chinese and he was a foreigner. Why cannot I make such sacrifices? I realized that at the beginning of the Cultural Revolution I had taken up an attitude of anarchism.

I did what I could whilst at work but after work I wanted to have nothing to do with the company. I studied Mao's 'Combat Liberalism' and carried many of my problems to the class when this was being discussed. In this work Chairman Mao describes eleven examples of liberal attitudes; I realized that many of these were directly applicable to myself and once I got them sorted out I became much more active in my work as well as ideologically. I became gay and at the same time the idea of discipline was planted in my head.

In my brigade I took the initiative and saw that I did my share of the work. I gave talks in my brigade to many of the older workers who, under the old society, had had no education, and I wrote letters for them.

Despite the short period of study I feel that I have already reaped a good harvest. I have been successful in my studies and now I have an honest attitude. But Chairman Mao has said that 'if we have a good theory but merely prate about it, pigeonhole it and do not put it into practice, then that theory, however good, is of no significance'.

I wish to follow these instructions. I wish to transform my ideology, to fight against egoism and at all times expose all my false ideas to my comrades. I wish to make sure that Chairman Mao's ideas should be dominant in my thinking.

Chairman Mao has said: 'The world is yours, as well as ours, but in the last analysis, it is yours. You young people, full of vigour and vitality, are in the bloom of life, like the sun at eight or nine in the morning. Our hope is placed on you. ... The world belongs to you. China's future belongs to you'.

I am only 26. I wish to serve the people with all my heart and soul and to be a successor of the revolution. I wished that the colour of our country should never change. I wish to be in accord with my comrades.

My life is limited but I wish to be an unlimited force.

A driver:

... Some of my comrades were members of the rebel group which took power in January. After power had been seized, the position of some of these comrades began to change. They wanted to take a car to go to meetings in town instead of going by bus. This was a bourgeois style; the old Director had done the same thing. We said: You have a new responsibility to the company, you cannot merely repeat what the old leaders did, we must fight against egoism even in the smallest thing; even in the case of cars. Our duty is to hold ourselves responsible to the people.

... In May 1967 the general situation in the company was good but there were still divergencies among the comrades themselves. Some suffered from small group mentality and on the other hand, the big groups were tending to throw their weight about. To resolve these questions we organized study at all levels. We succeeded in organizing five big meetings on the fight against egoism – they took all day. In the spirit of the five articles* we examined our actions and ideas. We focused on one question: 'If the situation is excellent why do we revolutionary groups small and large have these separate groups?' After this everyone understood that the fundamental task for all the organizations was a common one. At this time Chairman Mao had not made his statement, following the tour of northern and eastern cities. We took his statement that 'there can be no cause for conflict within the working class'. As a result we succeeded in getting rid of these differences.

A Factory for Blind and Deaf Workers

The Welfare State in the West has something of the condescending atmosphere of charity. The emphasis in China is not on helping the unfortunate, or even on helping them to help themselves, but rather on calling upon them to contribute something to building socialism. In every quarter of Shanghai there are factories employing blind and deaf-mute workers – those who were formerly an intolerable burden on some poor family, or who scratched a living as fortune tellers and beggars – the discarded scrap heap of a cruel society.

The factory which I visited in November 1967 was started

* The three most read articles are: 'Serve the People', 'In Memory of Norman Bethune', and 'The Foolish Old Man Who Removed the Mountains'. There have now been added for universal study 'How to Correct Mistaken Ideas in the Party' and 'On the Correct Handling of Contradictions among the People'.

in 1958 with four helpers, four blind workers and four deaf-mutes. They worked by hand with very simple equipment. Now there are 460 workers, of whom 130 are normal. The handicapped workers have succeeded in learning to manage mechanical equipment. The work is ingeniously arranged so that the blind can signal to the deaf by switching on a light when help is needed to repair a machine. The mutes communicate with the normal by finger language. The blind can not only read but also write by pricking out characters in a kind of Braille.

The Cultural Revolution penetrated even here. The workers felt that the Party branch was contaminated with the reactionary line. The management of the factory was undemocratic. The Secretary of the Party branch did not consult with the workers but behaved like an officer giving orders. The blind workers led a rebellion. At first the Party tried to repress them, but they came to the conclusion in the end that their cadres were not really anti-socialist, but had followed the Liu line out of mistaken loyalty. Now a Great Alliance had been formed and work was going ahead in a good spirit.

It was evident that in the problem of making unfortunate people feel that they are not rejected, that they can be of use not only to their own families but the nation, that they are playing a part in a grand movement, the Cultural Revolution is a great help. Every success in learning to overcome a handicap was not only an achievement for the individual, but a vindication of socialism and the Thought of Mao Tse-tung. The normal workers, also, whose tasks must sometimes be exasperating, were evidently buoyed up by the general release of spirits which the Cultural Revolution has brought about.

Educational Institutions, Peking and Shanghai

The indictment of the rebel students against the teaching that they were receiving was, first, that the courses were too long, too formal and too little directed to practical application; second, that the object of education was to build up an elite, divorced from the mass of the people; and third, that students from worker and peasant families were discriminated against instead of being helped to make up for their lack of literary background.

I

At the Geological Institute in Peking the old style of teaching was largely based on Soviet text books. The courses were highly theoretical, permitting little scope for field work. Political discussion was discouraged, and slavish loyalty to the Party was inculcated.

At the Medical Academy the teaching was intended to produce the elite of the profession but it was not at all well designed for that purpose. The course was of eight years; the first three were devoted to general science, and the fourth and fifth to pre-medical training; only in the last three years was any clinical work introduced. Emphasis was upon the individual patient and there was no discussion of the social aspects of medicine and its relation to politics.

At the College of Construction and Civil Engineering at Shanghai the students of architecture complained that they had to make drawings of Notre Dame in Paris, the Law Courts in London, ancient Chinese palaces, and that they were taught highfalutin theory, such as that a door both separates and joins two spaces. After a course of six years, it was necessary to have two years of practical work before they were of any use. Personal ambition to excel as an artist was inculcated. The freshman was told that an architect must have the brain of a philosopher, the eye of a painter, the ear of a musician and the soul of a poet. The students felt that they were being trained to serve an aristocracy, not to meet the urgent needs of the people.

The college was an old one which had been founded by Germans in 1907. With Liberation it had been enlarged and the style of teaching altered but much remained of the old tradition. The majority of teachers were bourgeois intellectuals, many of whom had been educated in the West. They controlled all the faculties and imposed their conceptions upon the courses.

In 1949 not more than 4 per cent of the students came from the families of workers and peasants, now there are more than 50 per cent. But the teachers discriminated against them and jeered at them. In the bourgeois atmosphere some students from poor homes, instead of being proud of proletarian origins, tried to conceal them. There was a pathetic tale of a lad whose mother pulled a cart refusing to recognize her when she came by the college.

Some of the younger teachers and some students had made several attempts to challenge the professors and to introduce Chairman Mao's ideas on education. They had some successes, but each time the old guard frustrated them and undid their reforms.

II

In these three institutions, and in many others, the course of the Cultural Revolution followed mainly the same lines, with individual variations.

The rebel movement began in June 1966, following the lead of Peking University, with posters criticizing the authorities.

At the Geological Institute a work team was sent in. The work team maintained that they were representing Chairman

Mao; it was only later that the students learned that they
were sent by Liu Shao-ch'i while Chairman Mao was not in
Peking. Next, the Ministry of Geology sent a team of two
hundred members, led by the Vice Minister. There was a
member of the Party Committee of the Institute who was on
the side of the rebel students. He organized a demonstration of
2,000 students against the work team and drove them out. A
new team was sent in by Po I-po, the Minister in charge of
economic affairs. (He was afterwards recognized as one of
the chief supporters of Liu Shao-ch'i and disgraced.) With
this authority behind it, the work team made a sharp attack
upon the rebel students. They branded those who opposed
them as counter revolutionaries. They demanded that the
rebels should make self-criticism. Many, confused and intimi-
dated, complied and wrote long self-criticisms. Party members
who had sided with the rebels were dismissed. Students were
forbidden to take part in national demonstrations. But the
leader of the rebels refused to submit and kept up the struggle.
This period of 'white terror' continued till the end of July,
when Mao returned to Peking and the work teams were recalled.

Now the students, encouraged by the publication of the
Sixteen Points, carried the war into the enemy camp. They
marched to the Ministry of Geology, chanting slogans against
the Vice Minister. A second march was organized on 5 September. More than a thousand students, and teachers who
sympathized with them, occupied the Ministry. The staff were
incited against the demonstrators, and cooks refused to feed
them. They camped in the Ministry for three days without
food. Their chief enemy, the Vice Minister, was dismissed.
(The Minister of Geology remains in office.) Red Guards com-
piled an indictment of Po I-po, which they believed to show
that he had been an anti-socialist at heart even before the
Liberation. (When asked how it was possible for a traitor to

remain hidden for so long, students replied that it took time to expose his crimes.)

In the Institute, out of 800 teachers only two or three were finally exposed as 'taking the capitalist road'. The rest, in the autumn of 1967, were accepted by the Red Guards and those who had first been hostile were admitting the necessity to change their ideas and methods of work.

At the Medical Academy events followed somewhat the same course, except that the Director, a world-famous surgeon, early accepted the rebels' criticism and came over to their side, so that he himself was attacked by other Party members in the administration of the Academy and by the work team sent in to quell the rebels, who branded him as a counter-revolutionary.

The movement began with a poster put up on 2 June criticizing the style of teaching in the Academy. A work team was sent in on 4 June; they convinced some students but the rebels succeeded in driving them out.

The reorganization of the Ministry of Propaganda on 25 June was an important victory for Chairman Mao's supporters at the level of national government, but unfortunately the new Vice Minister, Tau Chu (the Party Secretary for the Southern Region) who camouflaged himself as an ultra-leftist, turned out to be one of the most obstinate opponents of the Cultural Revolution.

He made a report to the Academy defending the Ministry of Health and accusing the rebels of opposing the Central Committee and taking a counter-revolutionary line. The students refused to applaud the report and shouted: 'Down with the top Party person taking the capitalist road.' They put up posters deriding Tau Chu. Some students, however, were taken in and sharp disputes broke out. The rebels encouraged each other, finding support in the book of quotations. They wrote a letter to Chairman Mao explaining the situation in the Academy.

When Mao returned to Peking the work team was withdrawn. After the publication of the Sixteen Points the students demanded that the work team should come back to submit to criticism and that Tau Chu should come back to answer for his report.

On 23 August he came back. Liu Shao-ch'i had not admitted defeat and was still encouraging the work teams who were trying to suppress the movement.

Tau Chu tried to protect the students and teachers who were opposing the rebels. The counter-revolutionaries had made a list of students who were active in the Cultural Revolution and whose names appeared on posters. Tau Chu castigated the rebels, not sparing the Director, whom he described as a cadre in the fourth category of the Sixteen Points – an anti-socialist Rightist who should be expelled from the Party.

The Sixteen Points vindicated the rebels, but the power of finance and administration was still in the hands of the reactionaries. They tried to frustrate the students by cutting off supplies of paper and ink for writing posters. On 11 November (which is winter in Peking) they ordered the staff to stop the heating and electricity and to close the canteen.

The students defiantly worked by candlelight and built themselves a 'protest stove' to cook their own meals. (This became known as the 11 November incident.) Such tactics only disillusioned students who had been deceived by the reactionaries. In a series of meetings in November the rebels gained a majority. The Party Secretary of the Institute was attacked and heavily criticized. (In the end, he was the only cadre to be condemned as 'taking the capitalist road'. In November 1967 he was in the stage of being 'given a chance to turn over a new leaf'.) At the end of June 1967 a Revolutionary Committee was set up on the basis of a Triple combination of cadres, revolutionary students and teachers and representatives of the students' militia.

The Director was now evidently on excellent terms with the rebels. He was a man with a sufficient sense of humour not to mind being taught to suck eggs by his young pupils and also with a sense of dedication which made him feel that their revolutionary enthusiasm could be harnessed to build up the kind of medical profession that China needs.

In Shanghai the students were not so much in the vanguard as they were in Peking; they followed and supported the workers and they played a part in the January Storm which led to the seizure of power in the City.

At the College of Construction there had been earlier attempts to reform education along the lines advocated by Chairman Mao; each time the movement was frustrated; the successes which had been gained were reversed and teaching relapsed into the old style. The Cultural Revolution was a great opportunity to try once more. A group of Red Guards was formed, at first with 700 members. It was countered by a conservative organization with 4,000 members, but as the struggle in the city raged through the summer and autumn of 1966, the rebel students gained adherents, and in December the conservative organization collapsed. Rebels seized power in the University. In June 1967 a committee took charge of the college under a chairman who was a student 23 years old.

In the autumn of 1967 their discussions of the reform of education were amongst the most advanced in the country, and were being published as an example to other institutions.

III

In the spring of 1967 many schools reopened but serious reorganization did not generally begin until the autumn, after another long summer holiday. When the students came back to academic work, most of the time was devoted to a discussion of how to embody the principles of the Cultural Revolution in education. Students have completely lost their old awe of professors, and some professors, though not opposing the new ideas, find it hard to accommodate to them. Some, however, like the Director of the Academy of Medicine, recognized the need for change and are helping to work out reforms. Many young teachers, moreover, wholeheartedly suported the students against the 'scholar tyrants' and the old mandarin style of teaching.

The main point is to make study more practical and to shorten courses so as to speed up the supply of young recruits to all professions, and at the same time to break down the concept of an educated man as a superior being to whom society owes more than to any simple worker.

At the Geological Institute classes had begun in the autumn of 1967 and students were undertaking revision to pick up the thread of their interrupted courses. At the same time discussions were going on, carrying out a critical review of the Soviet textbooks that were formerly in use, and making plans for a new system of selection to overcome the handicaps of workers' and peasants' children, and a new system of examinations with more emphasis on practical work and less on mere memory.

At the Academy of Medicine the discussion of the length of courses was still going on. There was general agreement that eight years was far too long, that book work should be cut down and that students should be brought into contact with the problems of peasants and workers and their families at an early stage in the curriculum. In the course of the Cultural Revolution there had been a great extension of the system of sending out medical teams from the cities to visit rural areas, giving a boost to the work of the health service in the communes. The proposal at the Academy was to send out students with the qualified doctors and surgeons, to observe their work, act as bottle-washers for them and become acquainted with the conditions of rural life. Returning to books and lectures, they would learn much faster when they had had some contact with reality. The system was already being tried out. Classes had begun; about one third of the time was being spent on formal teaching and two thirds on the study of application of the principles of the Cultural Revolution to the work of the Academy.

Chinese traditional treatments are studied along with modern medicine. In the countryside the older generation still have more confidence in them and some have been proved to produce cures which are still unexplained by science.

At the College of Construction at Shanghai, which had reassembled in July 1967, discussions on the same lines were going on. Education must be made more practical and oriented to meeting the needs of the people.

The earlier attempts at reform were being analysed to see what their purposes were and how they had been frustrated. Teams were being sent out to compare experiences with the most advanced institutions in Peking and into the country to find out the needs of the people and to get ideas from the peasants.

The proposal to combine research, teaching and production was criticized by some old-fashioned technicians with bourgeois ideas, who considered it Utopian but it was approved by the workers and peasants with whom the students discussed it.

A scheme was being worked out to reorganize the system of faculties so as to reduce the absolutism of the professors. The course was to be reduced from five years to three. In the first year, half the time would be devoted to productive work and militia training, half the time to basic theoretical studies. In the second year, two thirds of time should be spent on the study of design through practical work in the research institute. The third year should be devoted to the theory of a specialized subject and the design of a complete project in the appropriate field.

Methods of examination were being discussed. In some subjects, it was said, an examination was not necessary as the student could be judged on his general performance. In some, reference books should be used, so as to prevent an examination from being a mere test of memory. In some cases, several students might discuss their answers together and present a joint paper. In this way examinations would cease to be, as Mao put it, a surprise attack by the teachers on the students, and become a test of real proficiency.

Above all, the students were to be imbued with a new proletarian spirit, to overcome the bourgeois prejudices in which they had been infected in the past.

All this is still in the melting pot. It remains to be seen whether so much emphasis on politics will undermine the devotion to hard study which technicians cannot dispense with, or whether, as the Red Guards claim, it will on the contrary enhance it.

POSTSCRIPT

EIGHTEEN months after the period when these notes were taken, in April 1969, the Cultural Revolution was completed in a formal sense by the Ninth Congress of the Communist Party of China. In another sense it can never be completed for it sets out a line of development which is to be pursued indefinitely. Discussion, reorganization, and the struggle between 'two lines' is still going on.

In the summer of 1968, it seems, sharp political conflicts were still unresolved. There were sporadic outbursts of violence and even bloodshed, which the Western press was delighted to exaggerate, but in September it was announced that Revolutionary Committees had been established in all Provinces (except Taiwan, as the Chinese spokesmen are careful to add).

The history of this period was summarized in Lin Piao's address to the Congress*:

The struggle between the proletariat and the bourgeoisie for the seizure of power was a life-and-death struggle. During the one year and nine months from Shanghai's January storm of revolution in 1967 to the establishment of the revolutionary committees of Tibet and Sinkiang in September 1968, repeated trials of political strength took place between the two classes and the two lines, fierce struggles went on between proletarian and non-proletarian ideas and an extremely complicated situation emerged. As Chairman Mao has said: 'In the past, we fought north and south; it was easy to fight such wars. For the enemy was obvious. The present Great Proletarian Cultural Revolution is much more difficult than that kind of war. The problem is that those who commit ideological errors are mixed up with those whose con-

* See *Peking Review*, Special Issue, 28 April 1969.

tradiction with us is one between ourselves and the enemy, and for a time it is hard to sort them out.' Nevertheless, relying on the wise leadership of Chairman Mao, we finally overcame this difficulty. In the summer of 1967, Chairman Mao made an inspection tour north and south of the Yangtse River and issued extremely important instructions, guiding the broad revolutionary masses to distinguish gradually the contradictions between ourselves and the enemy from those among the people and to further bring about the revolutionary great alliance and the revolutionary three-in-one combination and guiding people with petty-bourgeois ideas on to the path of the proletarian revolution. Consequently, it was only the enemy who was thrown into disorder while the broad masses were steeled in the course of the struggle.

The handful of renegades, enemy agents, unreformed landlords, rich peasants, counter-revolutionaries, mad elements and rightists, active counter-revolutionaries, bourgeois careerists and double-dealers who had hidden themselves among the masses would not reveal their colours until the climate suited them. In the summer of 1967 and the spring of 1968, they again fanned up a reactionary evil wind to reverse correct verdicts both from the Right and the extreme 'Left'. They directed their spearhead against the proletarian headquarters headed by Chairman Mao, against the People's Liberation Army and against the new-born revolutionary committees. In the meantime, they incited the masses to struggle against each other and organized counter-revolutionary conspiratorial cliques in a vain attempt to stage a counter-seizure of power from the proletariat. However, like their chieftain Liu Shao-ch'i, this handful of bad people was finally exposed. This was an important victory for the Great Proletariat Cultural Revolution.

There was not only conflict with the enemies of the Cultural Revolution but also problems within the ranks of its supporters. All along the spontaneity of the movement had been held within certain limits. Mao Tse-tung's appeal to the people in general: 'To rebel is justified!; Occupy yourself with State affairs!; Go into the whys and wherefores!' and the appeal in the Sixteen Points: 'Trust the masses, rely on them and respect their initiative. . . . In the course of normal and full debate, the masses will affirm what is right, correct what is wrong and gradually reach unanimity'* mean that he had great faith in the basic common sense of the Chinese people. But from the first it was necessary to guard against the disruptive tendencies of individualism. The statement of Mao Tse-tung on the eve of Liberation was often quoted:

It is necessary resolutely to overcome certain manifestations of indiscipline or anarchy existing in many places. There are people who, without authorization, modify the policies and tactics adopted by the Central Committee or other higher Party committees and apply extremely harmful policies and tactics, which go against the united will and discipline but which they opinionatedly believe to be correct. There are also people who, on the pretext of pressure of work, adopt the wrong attitude of neither asking for instructions before an action is taken nor submitting a report afterwards and who regard the area they administer as an independent realm. All this is extremely harmful to the interests of the revolution. Party committees at every level must discuss this matter again and again and work earnestly to overcome such indiscipline and anarchy so that all the powers that can and must be centralized will be concentrated in the hands of the Central Committee and its agencies.†

The stress, in the period leading up to October 1968, was more upon the need for discipline than on the need for rebellion.

We must oppose the theory of 'many centres', that is the theory of 'no centre', mountain stronghold mentality, sectarianism and

---

* See pp. 88 and 90.
† See *Peking Review*, 30 June 1967.

all other reactionary bourgeois trends which undermine working class leadership.*

Even Liu Shao-ch'i was held up for reprobation as an advocate of anarchism. At the same time that he was being attacked and mocked for advocating slavish obedience to authority and maintaining that Party discipline requires commands to be carried out even when they are wrong, he was also accused of the opposite vice:

China's Khrushchev said, with ulterior motives: 'Do as the masses want' and 'mainly depend on the spontaneity of the mass movement'. Such statements as these plainly show how he opposed the Party leadership and peddled anarchism.†

There is no attempt to set such statements in their context (they were made, it seems, before Liberation) or to account for Liu Shao-ch'i's change of front. The quotation is not intended as a contribution to historical analysis. It is evidently provided to strengthen the hand of the moderate and sensible group in any organization in their arguments with a colleague who is carrying the injunction to defend his own opinions to unreasonable lengths.

This swing back to an emphasis upon discipline does not appear to be an inconsistency with the principles of 1966 but rather a natural development from their success.

The celebrations of October the First 1968 acclaiming the victory of the Cultural Revolution were followed by a meeting of the Central Committee. A communique adopted on 31 October 1968 was evidently intended to wind up the period of struggle. It finally named Liu Shao-ch'i by his name and announced his expulsion from the Party (nothing has been said about the fate of the man, as opposed to the symbolic figure); and it announced the decision to hold the Party Congress.

The Congress opened on 1 April 1969. Lin Piao, now Vice-Chairman and the accepted successor to Chairman Mao, gave

* Hsinhua News Agency, 11 August 1968.
† Hsinhua News Agency, 15 March 1968.

the main address, recounting the history of the Cultural Revolution and stressing the main themes – leniency to opponents who admit their errors and re-education of bourgeois academics; the need to maintain vigilance in the continuing struggle between the 'two lines'; the re-establishment of the Party – 'getting rid of the stale and taking in the fresh'; and solidarity with all the peoples of the world (including the people of the Soviet Union) in their struggles against oppression. On the question of world war, he quoted a pregnant saying of Chairman Mao: 'There are but two possibilities: one is that war will give rise to revolution and the other is that revolution will prevent war.'

In the celebrations and discussions following the Congress the emphasis has been upon unity and reconciliation but also upon the need to carry the movement forward and 'never forget class struggle'.

The new constitution of the Party is designed to embody the style of work and of relations with the people that emerged from the rebellion.

Leading bodies of the Party at all levels shall regularly report on their work to congresses or general membership meetings, constantly listen to the opinions of the masses both inside and outside the Party and accept their supervision. Party members have the right to criticize Party organizations and leading members at all levels and make proposals to them. If a Party member holds different views with regard to the decisions or directives of the Party organizations, he is allowed to reserve his views and has the right to bypass the immediate leadership and report directly to higher levels, up to and including the Central Committee and the Chairman of the Central Committee. It is essential to create a political situation in which there are both centralism and democracy, both discipline and freedom, both unity of will and personal ease of mind and liveliness.*

* From Article 5 of the Constitution of the Communist Party of China. See *Peking Review*, 30 April 1969.

Whatever disturbances there may have been in the course of the Cultural Revolution, economic development seems to have been running on. The harvest for 1968 was reported to be good once more; in some industries there have been setbacks due to disturbances, but in many there are claims of new technical advances, increased production, savings in costs and improvements in quality due to the simplified organization and high morale that the Cultural Revolution brought into the factories. The Western businessmen who attend the trade fair in Canton report that conditions appear to be normal from their point of view.

In the reform of education there have been fresh developments. A number of investigations have been made into the performance of students after completing their training, of which one has been widely publicized. This is concerned with the criticism of the Shanghai Institute of Mechanical Engineering made by the workers and staff of an important machine tool plant. The conclusion (with which many Western industrialists would sympathize) is that the best engineers are those who had some practical experience before taking university courses and that education should be integrated with practical work and with research.*

Mao Tse-tung commented on this report:

It is still necessary to have universities; here I refer mainly to colleges of science and engineering. However, it is essential to shorten the length of schooling, revolutionize education, put proletarian politics in command and take the road of the Shanghai Machine Tools Plant in training technicians from among the workers. Students should be selected from among workers and peasants with practical experience, and they should return to production after a few years' study.†

Similarly, the members of communes were asked to give

* Hsinhua Supplement (13), September 1968.
† *Peking Review*, 2 August 1968.

their views on the students who have been sent to work with them:

The poor and lower-middle peasants pointed out that in the past what the schools put into practice was the principle that 'intellectual training comes first' and 'marks comes first'. This meant 'recognizing the marks only but not persons, still less the social classes people belong to'. Many pupils were forced to be 'preoccupied with marks while looking at their books'. In school, they strove for marks, and when working in the brigade they strove for 'marks, marks, marks', and as a result the revolution was completely displaced and thrown to the four winds.*

An enlightening remark is quoted from the mother of a soldier. 'Now we are striving to build socialist new villages, we need many talented people. But what we don't want are college students who are divorced from proletarian politics and practice and who look down upon the labouring people.' The struggle against the mandarin tradition cannot succeed in a day.

A new system has been introduced to put schools in the rural areas under the control of the brigades in the Communes so as to direct education to what the peasants consider useful. (No doubt some of the old style teachers do not find it easy to adapt themselves to this situation.) At the end of 1968 there was a great movement of young high school and college graduates into the villages to 'integrate themselves with the people' and assist in the application of science to production – a contribution to the long-term policy of breaking down the 'three great differences' between town and country, between intellectual and manual work, and between agriculture and industry.

Urban schools are brought into connexion with industrial enterprises. The pupils carry on 'part work, part study' and the workers educate the teachers.

* ibid, p. 22.

In many universities and colleges it seems that the attempts at reform led to long wrangles which sometimes broke out into disorder and led to buildings being damaged and apparatus being smashed up. The remedy was found in sending in propaganda teams of workers and soldiers which, it is claimed, brought the hostile groups together in discussions lasting sometimes a few days, sometimes a few weeks, and set the new course of education going.

In the medical field, the ideas discussed at the Academy in 1967* were being pressed. In many communes, health workers with an introductory training are encouraged to get experience (passing difficult cases to the regular clinics) working in their own villages, and a selection is made from amongst them for training in medical colleges.

These developments are logical. If the Party and the intellectuals are to *serve the people,* the people must judge the service, though Western professors secure in their 'mountain strongholds' would not much like the judgement to be applied to themselves.

* See p. 144.

MORE ABOUT PENGUINS
AND PELICANS

Penguin Book News, which appears every month, contains details of all the new books issued by Penguins as they are published. From time to time it is supplemented by *Penguins in Print* a complete list of all our available titles. (There are well over three thousand of these.)

A specimen copy of *Penguin Book News* will be sent to you free on request, and you can become a subscriber for the price of the postage – 4s. for a year's issue (including the complete lists). Just write to Dept EP, Penguin Books Ltd, Harmondsworth, Middlesex, enclosing a cheque or postal order, and your name will be added to the mailing list.

Some other Pelicans are described on the following pages.

Note: *Penguin Book News* and *Penguins in Print* are not available in the U.S.A. or Canada

THE BIRTH OF COMMUNIST CHINA

C. P. Fitzgerald

This Pelican, which is a fully revised edition of the author's *Revolution in China*, sets out to assess the significance of the Chinese Revolution.

After sketching in the background of China's long history and social structure C. P. Fitzgerald, who is now Professor of Far Eastern History at Canberra, opens his main account at the fall of the Manchu Emperors in 1911 and traces the origins of revolution through the early republic of Sun Yat-sen and the Nationalist dictatorship of Chiang Kai-shek to the military campaigns of Mao Tse-tung. He assesses the varying influences of Confucianism and Christianity, of East and West, and of the Japanese and Russians on this massive movement, and makes it abundantly clear that the China of today is not an inexplicable freak but a logical development of its immensely long past.

Professor Fitzgerald has a gift for fluent narrative and a long experience of China, and his interpretation of one of the central political events of this century is as readable as it is reliable.

POLITICAL LEADERS OF THE
TWENTIETH CENTURY

MAO TSE-TUNG

Stuart Schram

By any reckoning Mao Tse-tung must be regarded as
one of the greatest and most remarkable statesmen of
modern times. As a poet of distinction, as a political
philosopher of major importance, and as a strategist whose
6000-mile trek across China has become a legend, Mao
has devoted his life to China and the Chinese peasants.
Indeed the Chinese People's Republic has shaped a whole
pattern of revolution for poor peasant societies. In this new
biography Stuart Schram sifts fact from fiction in the long
story of Mao's struggle to free the greatness of China and
to give a new meaning to Marxism.

POLITICAL LEADERS OF THE
TWENTIETH CENTURY

These political biographies will analyse in depth the real
men lurking behind the personality cults of great contemporary statesmen. Their purpose is to explain how such
political leaders of our times as Mao Tse-tung and Mac-
millan, de Gaulle and Stalin, Lenin and Verwoerd formed
their political outlooks, to examine how they gained power
and how they held and exercised it, and to suggest what
each of them has come to epitomize in the eyes of his own
nation and of the world at large.

Also by Joan Robinson

ECONOMIC PHILOSOPHY

This exceptionally stimulating book begins by showing how the basic human need for a morality on which the conscience can work has led to the necessity for a philosophy of economics in any society. It is stressed that economic values and money values are not identical and it is the task of the economist to justify the image of Mammon to man 'not to tell us what to do, but show why what we are doing anyway is in accord with proper principles'. The relations between science and ideology over the last two hundred years are traced from Adam Smith, through Marx and Keynes, to the dichotomy that exists in current economic thinking and the pressing fundamental problems which must now be faced.

'It would be difficult to think of a better book than this to place in the hands of the reader who thinks that economics is simply a matter of statistics, and who needs to be convinced of its intellectual interest and excitement' – Samuel Brittan in the *Observer*

NOT FOR SALE IN THE U.S.A.